SPANIELS FOR SPORT

Spaniels for Sport

by

TALBOT RADCLIFFE

based on H. W. Carlton's classic
Spaniels: Their Breaking for
Sport and Field Trials

with a Foreword by
Wilson Stephens
editor of *The Field*

FABER AND FABER
3 Queen Square
London

First published in 1969
by Faber and Faber Limited
3 Queen Square London WC1
Reprinted 1972 and 1975
Printed in Great Britain by
Latimer Trend & Company Ltd Plymouth

ISBN 0 571 08772 8

Dedicated to
Field Trial Champion
SAIGHTON'S STINGER

With grateful acknowledgements to

The Harmsworth Press Ltd for the use of H. W. Carlton's work *Spaniels: Their Breaking for Sport and Field Trials*.

To Rosslyn and Rosie for cheerful encouragement

To Don Williams and Major J. A. Pearce for some excellent photography

Contents

Contents

Contents

Illustrations

All the photographs are by Don Williams with the exception
of No.1, which is by Major J. A. Pearce; No.4d which is by
C. M. Cooke & Son; No.6b, which is by A. L. Lennie.

Foreword

by Wilson Stephens

In the wide literature of dog training no book has been more widely accepted as a classic than H. W. Carlton's *Spaniels, Their Breaking for Sport and Field Trials*. In Britain and America, and wherever else English is spoken and spaniels work to the gun, it has long been a standard work. Its language is simple, its reasoning lucid, its insight into dog and man both clear and charitable. It may well be asked, Why add anything to a work so perfect in its own original form? And by what right does Talbot Radcliffe set out to gild this lily?

Carlton first published this little masterpiece in 1915, more than half a century ago. Much has changed since then and in this context the significant changes are the effect of the intervening years on men, gundogs, and sport. Examinations of them will reveal whether there was a need for Carlton's text to be re-fitted to modern times.

First then, the men. Although Carlton's first publication was in 1915, his writing establishes (as would anyway be obvious) that his ideas reflect the conditions of Edwardian England as a country gentleman knew them. The limitless time, the unthinkability that business might ever interfere with pleasure, the spacious backgrounds in which no man lacked paddocks nor access to coverts well stocked with whatever game the lesson of the moment demanded. From sunrise to sundown nothing of the workaday world seemed to intrude upon a man intent on training a spaniel. Not so now. Gundogs not professionally trained are trained by men busy in other ways; too busy in most cases to give the slowly maturing care which Carlton assumed would invariably be available; too busy also to afford to dispense with the short cuts in diagnosis and reasoning by which Radcliffe has made the Carlton doctrine more easy to apply.

Next, the dogs. Half a century covers at least 15 dog-generations. In human terms this represents the difference between Man as he was when printing was invented, and Man as he is in the space age. Mental aptitudes sharpen, verve and drive are concentrated. The spaniel of today is that much nearer the reality of the thoroughbred horse, and that much further away from the stolid, common stock out of which it was forged. Field trials have developed ever greater pace, and by sensitising the canine mind made its reflexes even more delicate and amenable. The keenness of a highly-bred modern spaniel comes very near to being a fieriness which man must master combined with a gentleness which 'heavy hands' must never bruise. Though this was also true in Carlton's day, and certainly he knew it, the intervening years have heightened and deepened its significance. Few would doubt that if he were alive now Carlton himself would have extra thoughts to add on the question of temperament and the man-dog relationship which it permits. Not for nothing has Radcliffe varied the order of the Carlton canon by making Psychology his first chapter. Carlton made it last but one.

Thirdly, the sport. In the cumulative heritage of the spaniel race, the work they do has changed little for 2,000 years. In Roman times their ancestors hunted up and sprang game for falconers. In the years before gunpowder they combined this with springing game into nets (for long the general way of obtaining partridges, pheasants, and many wildfowl for the table). For them, springing game to the gun has not been very different. The changes have been man-made, and man-felt. Through man's action (by spreading the disease, myxomatosis) Britain temporarily and almost completely lost the rabbit. This piece of history is likely to repeat itself in other countries. In terms both of training and of shooting tactics, the present generation of shooters have needed to re-think the techniques of employing spaniels. Carlton did not and could not foresee this. Nor could he have foreseen the increased popularity of wildfowling, and the part spaniels would play in it.

Hence the form of this re-edition of his memorable work. Hence, too, this Introduction to it. For two reasons the present writer would otherwise have been unwilling to stand between the reader and the text.

In the first place, Radcliffe needs no fanfare. He can stand by himself, as Carlton does. Most people know of his fidelity to his own strain of English springer spaniels, and of the repeated successes he has achieved with them. The championship honours both of Britain and America have gone to him. He has the stature (and few could claim it) to re-present Carlton to the sporting world. As editor of *The Field*, which published Carlton's original book and still holds its copyright, it is my duty and my pleasure to say that he does so with the complete confidence of the present proprietors.

In the second place the introduction to Carlton's text was written by no less a person than William Arkwright, whose own book on the pointer will be quoted as long as bird dogs quest for the gun, and who was a towering authority on all gundogs. To stand where better men have stood is not a posture to be adopted without good cause. My hope is that these explanatory lines constitute their own *raison d'être*. Nothing now remains but to leave the subject to Mr. Radcliffe and Mr. Carlton (with Mr. Arkwright not forgotten).

Introduction

I am delighted to have the opportunity of revising Mr. Carlton's remarkable book on dog training and of contributing further chapters.

His psychological approach is so realistic and so applicable to all breeds that if widely circulated throughout the world I believe it will become standard training practice for all amateurs, especially novices or beginners making their early attempt at dog training. If the general principles of psychology are applied to any breed at approximately the age advocated many heart-breaking experiences will be avoided, and pets, working gundogs, field trial and obedience test aspirants alike will greatly benefit.

Mr. Carlton was in a position to partake to the full of conditions more favourable than those of today and was highly intelligent in applying his experience and knowledge for the benefit of generations of would-be trainers. At times his explanations and expositions leave me marvelling at his wonderful grasp of the necessary essentials to training the perfect dog. He obviously had a wealth of experience of actual breeding and day to day handling so anyone following his teaching will gain many hours of satisfaction and pleasure in producing a good dog. I believe this book to be unique in that while it is devoted entirely to the training and education of the dog, the author also enlightens the would-be trainer himself.

His first-hand knowledge enabled him to emphasize the

'development of natural ability' as opposed to 'training' by intensive discipline—thereby producing a happy, gay, hard-working dog full of joie de vivre'. The modern working dog has been bred to possess great natural working gifts of intelligence, nose and mouth together with a real willingness to please. The clever and successful trainer encourages at all times the gradual development of these assets which lie dormant in the raw material he handles. In the original introduction to this book William Arkwright expressed this all-important point so well that I quote in full:

'Which are those qualities that the most capable master cannot put into his pupil? and without which no dog can become a firstrater—I will enumerate them here, so that they may be kept in mind right through the educational course.

1. *Docility*, which is the wish to learn—the desire to please his master.
2. *Courage*, which makes a dog unconscious of fatigue—which will crash him through the thickest cover—will force him across a river in flood.
3. *Nose* which really stands for keenness of scenting power combined with the sense to apply it aright.
4. *Style* which is chiefly merry bustle, with flashing tail, head ever erect—now high to reach a body scent, now low to investigate a foot scent—attributes that are most precious to a tired man or to one vexed by a bad shot. *Style* also exhibits itself in work of a decisive, dashing kind. For instance in springing game with such vehemence as to frighten it into leaving its covert posthaste.

The above are the purely natural qualities, which I believe to be hereditary—which are certainly impossible of inculcation by any trainer.'

This is a wonderful outline and description of Natural Ability. I would mention one additional natural quality:
Retrieving. A bold fast approach—a quick, confident pick-up —an uninterrupted return. A good mouth, inherent, is

essential to success, otherwise you have to force-retrieve, a method which I do not employ myself and which is best left to the specialist expert.

Mr. Carlton had little opportunity for water work so I have added a chapter on this important aspect of dog training. In addition I have dealt separately with teaching a dog to jump. This is very necessary now that so much barbed-wire is used for fencing on sporting properties. Barbed wire was much less used when this book was originally written and in the foxhunting 'Shires' where Carlton lived would have been virtually unknown.

Considering this revision, I felt that some illustrations would help to explain various aspects outlined in the book. I decided to contribute further chapters on Breeding and Puppies and Spaniels for Team Work. The present shortage of beaters on shooting days and consequent expense, makes the role of spaniels more and more important to the production of game on set shooting days. The handler or trainer who wishes to subsidise his sport with a small income can provide himself with much fun and his dogs with useful experience by Lending a Hand. Under this heading I am including a chapter on the correct procedure for picking-up on big days (see page 118).

In concluding my Introduction, I would like to record my own condensed generalizations.

Making yourself the 'centre of interest' to your pupil is the most important aspect of all training.

A dog must be healthy to be happy, and happy to be trained.

Let common sense control your progress.

Some have an innate gift for handling and training, others have not.

Cultivate and improve your own understanding of your dog's mind and temperament.

Learn to be sympathetic, to be tolerant but firm.

Be fair and consistent at all times.

Don't expect wonders from a youngster. They learn from continual repetition of each lesson.

Don't overdo retrieving—actual or practice.

Dropping to shot is the basis of steadiness in the field.

Avoid teaching your dog the power of the gun until it is steady, or at least until it is under reasonable control, (i.e. not running in to the fall).

Bad habits are to be avoided like the plague.

Developing faults are usually attributable to mistakes by the trainer.

Be observant. The impressionable age to establish training is five to eighteen months old. Earlier if possible.

Jealousy is a two-edged sword, but it can prove profitable with uncertain retrievers.

A natural retriever is a gem beyond price.

Don't take the sparkle away by overtraining.

Take time to finish.

Let natural ability develop at its own pace but always under control.

At no time must punishment be connected with the physical act of retrieving. If it is a faulty delivery will result.

At all times offer praise and encouragement. Never be harsh or temperamental; this can be disastrous.

Be just in punishment and avoid loss of temper.

Hunting a brace or team is a great thrill. Also it is great fun.

Avoid artificial aids if possible. Nobody is clever enough to deceive a youngster consistently.

The pupil should learn to be a success, and should expect to be a success. It will then be a success, because success breeds success.

PART ONE

Psychology

I

Psychology Before Training

*'Under domestication we seek to bring about a new
working adjustment to conditions imposed by man'*

In training a dog, whether a gundog or not, it must be remembered that although the aim of dog training is the control of the bodily actions, this can only be effected through
the medium of the dog's mind. It is, therefore, the mind and
not the body of the dog with which we are primarily concerned.

Handlers are unanimous in insisting that training must be
adapted to each dog's particular character and disposition:
one dog is shy, another bold; one is highly strung, another
stolid; one responsive, another self-centred; one docile,
another wilful; each must be treated with his characteristics
in view. These are all matters for the personal observation of
the individual handler to use in planning his training programme.

Some handlers seem incapable of training for steadiness or
obedience, or even preventing a trained dog from becoming
unsteady or disobedient. This may well be due to their
failure to become a centre of interest to the dog and thus
modify the predominant interest represented by Game. The
factors which go to make the handler the centre of interest
to the dog I am unable to suggest; if, however, the training is
not of an absorbing interest to the trainer himself, then it
seems improbable that he in turn will be a centre of interest
to the dog he is training. If he does not watch his dog, his dog

23

will never watch him. Possibly, too, this interaction of 'centres of interest' may account for some dogs being specially difficult to train; in their cases game may be so overmastering a 'centre of interest' at first as to leave no room for the trainer being of any interest whatsoever.

In the presence of more than one 'centre of interest', behaviour is entirely different to that which is evident in the presence of only one. This matter is considered of importance by scientists, many of whom argue that it affords an explanation of what at first appear to be cases of 'reflective imitation' ('the mirror of his master') (see page 33). In training, too, it should not be overlooked and should be considered in connection with complex situations that arise and develop in the course of training.

It is evident that the dam is always the centre of interest to unweaned pups. After weaning, food takes the place of the dam, thus creating a new centre of interest. At this stage a clever handler introduces himself, through food or feeding, as the new and permanent centre of interest. However as adolescence develops, gundogs will always create a centre of interest in Game and Game scents; this is a required natural development which has to be carefully controlled to enable the trainer to retain the position of chief centre of interest in the dog's mind while control and hunting instincts are being established.

In the case of social animals (primeval dogs lived in packs) the members of the group are centres of interest to each other. It is therefore most important that the successful trainer must become the CHIEF centre of interest to the dog he is training, competing for its interest against the other members of the litter. Possibly this is more readily achieved if he feeds the dog himself. If you start handling a puppy as soon as it is weaned, you introduce yourself as an interest before interest becomes centred in the rest of the litter. If and when you subsequently kennel the pupil by himself, you prevent a division of interest and attract the dog's attention and interest to yourself. Solitary kennelling is widely advocated. The reason given is that the dog is thus in a better position to think over and digest with undivided attention lessons it receives; in addition it develops self confidence at a much earlier age as it has learnt to rely on its own devices.

Never give a lesson unless you have the pupil's whole attention, or continue one when you have lost it. This injunction is, perhaps, the most important of all. It is absolutely essential that the pupil should have his entire attention concentrated on you, on your commands and the response you wish him to connect with such commands. If his attention is attracted elsewhere, your lesson will be useless. Most, if not all the best trainers, attach so much importance to this point that they never dream of giving a lesson when a third party is present, or in a spot where counter attractions are likely to present themselves; i.e. interesting scents, other dogs, fouled ground, other animals, children or spectators.

Lack of attention may arise from various circumstances. It may be caused by the puppy's state of mind. Its capacity for giving the necessary attention (see pages 23, 41) may well be impaired by fear of the trainer, by ill-health (see page 122), by boredom or by exhaustion. The first of these emphasizes yet again the importance of preserving good relations between yourself and your pupil. Most highly strung dogs, moreover, require quiet handling; if you shout to enforce your commands, their tails go down—(and the tail is a sure barometer of mood and feelings). Such dogs appear to lose their heads and become incapable of responding to your commands—in fact they mentally panic. So important a factor in their experiments do scientists regard this matter of attention, that it has been suggested that puppies should be subjected to a course of training in the HABIT of giving attention, and I cannot help thinking that the handbreaking lessons suggested later are of value, not only in teaching the specific matters set out, but also affording some general course of training the dog in Giving Attention as suggested above, thereby creating the right atmosphere to absorb tuition.

In all pursuits, the tendency of the dog is to search for reasons, and an enquiry into them might be of interest in itself. The application of reason may well be of practical value as an explanation for the occasional non-success of the old empirical methods (breaking instead of training), and suggest to the trainer original and possibly more successful methods of his own.

The trainer of dogs, dealing as he does with the dog's mind on the plane of its natural tendencies and its predominant interests, is in a far better position to observe certain phases in its development than the scientists whose observations are usually made on animals under the conditions of experiment and so of unnatural restraint. Under domestication we seek to bring about a new working adjustment to conditions imposed by man. The skilful trainer utilizes instinctive tendencies as a basis, encouraged by a system of rewards and (when necessary) punishments which leads to the intelligent modification of behaviour along the lines directed by his deliberate purpose.

Psychologists generally allow to animals the possession of intelligence but deny or do not admit the possession of reason. They hesitate, however, to assert that in no animals are there the beginnings of a rational scheme. So far as their observations on animals under test conditions go, the majority of psychologists draw a sharp distinction between the lower or *intelligent* stage of mental development and the higher or *rational* stage. They define intelligence as the power to learn by experience, they use the word 'reason' as pointing to something more than this, namely the power to found upon experience, and appreciate and apply a general scheme. Intelligence may enable a dog or a horse, by an extended series of trials and errors, to learn to open a particular gate or door, but it would require the exercise of reason to enable it to appreciate the fact that the latch of a door is the crucial point, and so be in a position to open all gates or doors provided with any ordinary latch. The same distinction may be applied to the processes of the human mind: 'If to prevent a boy sucking his thumb we administer bitter aloes, we trust to *intelligent* control through the immediate effect of experience, but if he be induced to give up the habit because it is babyish he so far exercises *rational* control' (Lloyd Morgan).

The meaning of the expressions used in this book will, I hope, be made reasonably clear; the next step is to enquire as to the mental material on which the trainer has to work. This would appear to consist of:

1. Instinct   3. Attention
2. Intelligence   4. Emotions

INSTINCT is an inherited tendency in the nature of a blind undiscriminating impulse, and its first exercise must necessarily be prior to the individual's experience, i.e. an experience on which the impulse could have been said to be based. Its characteristics appear to be:

(a) It may be, and in almost all cases is, modified by experience.

(b) It may not show itself until the animal has reached a certain age; in such a case it is called 'deferred', and this is quite common.

(c) Its development may be retarded by disuse or misuse.

(d) If it does not meet with satisfaction, it may, in the individual, gradually wane and disappear.

(e) The less deeply ingrained it is (and the more easily modified in the hands of the trainer) the sooner it lapses, and the more practice it requires to become a habit.

Very little consideration will be needed to see what a wealth of suggestion the above affords to the trainer. Take for instance 'chasing' (breaking or bolting out of control), the bugbear of many trainers and the downfall of many a good dog. Personally, I have never come across a young puppy that would chase the first rabbit or bird it saw. In my experience therefore, the impulse to chase is a 'deferred' impulse. Is it not then possible to prevent it ever manifesting itself?

Is it too far-fetched to suggest that dropping (i.e. sitting or standing) whenever a rabbit or bird moves may thus displace the innate impulse to chase, that the dropping impulse, though still undisplayed, is modified by the puppy's experience in the rabbit pen, that finally the reward and the pleasure of the trainer make dropping or sitting a more satisfactory response to the movement of the rabbit or bird than a chase?

There are other instances of 'deferred' instincts. I always test my young pups as to their retrieving or carrying capacity before they are 10 weeks old, and at the first attempt have invariably found that they will dash out for a knotted handkerchief (thrown only a short distance), immediately pick it up and come straight back with it. The earliest age at which this has been accomplished is five weeks. At that age, the pup, however keen he might ultimately become, showed no inclination to hunt or seek game and would not even acknowledge the line of a rabbit or scent of game that had just moved away. It would seem, therefore, that the hunting or seeking instinct is a 'deferred' instinct. One would have thought that an animal must catch a thing before it can carry it. This is puzzling until it is pointed out that a vixen would bring a rabbit to the earth, dismember it, then leave the cubs to carry off, fetch or retrieve their portions.

May not this also afford some answer to the question why some dogs are more difficult to train than others? The chasing or breaking instinct may be deeply ingrained, and so be the more difficult to cast out; the hunting/seeking, or carrying instinct may be slight, and so the more practice be required to attain perfection; the tendency to a hard mouth (if it can be classed as instinctive) may not be deeply ingrained, and so be the more easily modified.

INTELLIGENCE equates with learning by experience. A distinction has been drawn between 'intelligence' and 'reason' as these terms are understood by the majority of psychologists. Intelligence has also apparently to be distinguished from a lower form of experience, learning as an automaton. This latter form of experience-learning does not seem to carry the animal beyond the actual labyrinth in which it learnt, while in contrast good gundogs must be readily adaptable as they have to work on various grounds and under divers conditions.

In what way then does intelligence, in the sense of experience-learning work? It works in exactly the way that common sense would lead us to expect, i.e. all those actions that are accompanied or closely followed by pleasure or satisfaction, including success, are *stamped in* (by reward or encouragement), whereas actions accompanied by or closely followed by discomfort or displeasure, including non-success, are *stamped out* (by punishment or scolding).

In training, a similar process goes on, but as we have or ought to have an organized scheme, ourselves selecting the situation (e.g. a rabbit or bird moving off) and selecting the responses we desire (e.g. dropping or sitting), and have at our command the means of creating satisfaction or inflicting discomfort at will, the matter is to that extent simplified. Whether, however, the animal entirely teaches itself or is taught by us, the following matters are material:

(a) The association in the dog's mind of satisfaction with the response we desire to encourage and discomfort with the response we desire to inhibit.

(b) The amount of satisfaction or discomfort experienced.

(c) The closeness in point of time and the preciseness of connection between the response and the satisfaction or discomfort.

(d) The frequency with which the response we desire is connected with the given situation and the duration of each such connection.

(e) The readiness of the response to be connected with the situation.

(f) The fact that to a dog a 'situation' is at first a complex matter, consisting of many elements in addition to the one element to which you are teaching him to give the desired response.

(g) It is easier to obtain the response you desire *de novo*, than to get rid of a response already established and form a new one.

I fear that the above sounds terrifyingly obscure, but trust that the comments and instances immediately following may afford some measure of illumination. The first question that naturally arises is as to the comparative advantage of stamping in the desired response by satisfaction (such as a reward), or stamping out all other responses by discomfort (such as punishment). A consideration of (c) above, will afford a partial answer to the question.

Your spaniel breaks in to a very strong running cock-pheasant, hunts it up and returns triumphantly to you with the pheasant in its mouth. In lieu of the approval it expects, the dog is met with chastisement or hard words; the last thing it has done is to retrieve to hand, and it is undoubtedly the retrieving to hand and not the running-in (breaking) to shot, that your chastisement, if often repeated, would stamp out, leaving the running in possibly unaffected.

So, too, the chastisement of a dog that comes back to your whistle after a prolonged chase is neither sufficiently closely nor precisely connected with the running-in (breaking) to steady him, whereas, if he had been made to drop and been rewarded, both the conditions of closeness and precision would have been fulfilled. Moreover, rewarding for good behaviour rather than chastising for bad is far more likely to preserve the good relations between you and your dog, on which the success of your training so much depends.

My advocacy of stamping in the desired response is, of course, not intended to be universal. It applies, in my opinion, to the education of young puppies. In the case of older dogs that have already contracted bad habits, such as chasing or running in to shot, the trainer will perforce be thrown back upon stamping out; in these cases, 'spinning' the culprit when in full flight with the check-cord, hauling him back and dropping him, should effect a cure; it satisfies the conditions of closeness and preciseness which subsequent chastisement can never do; it also prevents the possibility of that most awkward of breaking puzzles, your action if a dog runs in and retrieves to hand.

As our training is analogous to the formation of a habit, no comment is needed upon the necessity of frequently connecting the response (say dropping) with the given situation (say a rabbit or bird moving off). On this point scientists moreover tell us that a slightly satisfying response made often may win a closer connection than a more satisfying response made only rarely. If this is effective in stamping in any desired response, it would appear to be equally true for stamping out responses we desire to inhibit, and correspond with the practice of most trainers who prefer to have a dog out for a short time every day rather than have him out for seven times as long on one day and then leave him for a week.

The duration of the connection, too, needs little comment. We all know that if a dog drops to shot and is IMMEDIATELY sent to retrieve, he will soon give up dropping and run-in (break).

The readiness of the response to be connected with the situation is most strongly emphasized in the case of forming a connection between going out to retrieve and 'fetch it' or some similar command. It is also at the root of the statement that a dog turns more readily to your whistle if he sees that you are working him across to game-holding cover.

It cannot be too strongly emphasized that the trainer

31

must at all times have everything connected with his training clear-cut and well defined in the mind of his dog. Animal consciousness has been described as a 'big blooming buzzing confusion', and it rests with the trainer to reduce this to orderliness by segregating and clarifying the situations and responses he desires.

It is a common experience that a dog may be perfectly steady when handled by its trainer, but wild with an unfamiliar purchaser, and, if the purchaser is a bad handler, continue wild to the end of the chapter. It is, moreover, common knowledge among trainers, that a spaniel may consistently drop to a moving rabbit in a pen and yet chase the first one that moves off outside it. The explanation of the last phenomenon, and a similar reasoning applies to the other two, appears to be this: in the mind of the trainer, the situation in the pen to which the dog responds by dropping is the rabbit and that alone; in the dog's mind, however, the situation is a compound one, consisting not only of the particular rabbit, but also of the trainer, the pen itself, the bushes it contains, the wire enclosing it, and maybe a hundred elements. It is only by keeping and varying the other elements of the situation that these two alone come to form a situation, to which the dog gives the desired response.

Comments on Chapter 1

In revising this book, I have purposely brought this chapter from the rear to the fore, as I attach so much importance to the human approach to the many involved problems that can arise. By intelligent self-appraisal, bad habits that form in early training can be avoided. This is, of course, the secret of successful training, reducing the whole procedure to its simplest form. Therefore, common sense, psychology and personal thinking in respect of each pupil must come first, as the first step must be your own introduction to the pupil.

So much the better if this is the first human contact the dog has made. You can then immediately create your own image to the pupil who will quickly respond, accepting the principle that you have become the centre of interest in its life, his lord and master. This to my mind is the most important period—the initial marriage, the humanization, the honeymoon. The build-up of confidence, before any serious training whatsoever commences, is essential. It is the sparring period in the opening rounds when the pupil is probing and feeling for his master's weaknesses—these when found by the dog will be exploited to the full. Hence faults develop in the dog, simply because the trainer has not paused to consider whether perhaps his actions and not the pupil's have produced a bad developing or recurring habit. This is where reflective imitation comes into the picture, the dog becomes a mirror of his master. It is why so many young dogs finish their training closely reflecting the personality of their trainer. It therefore behoves the trainer himself to study carefully his own personality as well as the dog's before proceeding too far with the training of his pupil, in case he may need to remedy unwanted characteristics in himself rather than in the dog—such as being too hasty, slow, jumpy, calm, confident, gay or dull. All these characteristics, including the desirable ones, if possessed to excess, can undermine efficiency in man or dog.

Training should proceed evenly. I like to think that a pup has no idea it is being trained for the first two months, say from 12 to 16/20 weeks old. Without realizing it the pupil will daily form habits that are the natural cornerstones of the foundation on which you will build, such as coming immediately when called, turning willingly to whistle at exercise, returning to hand with a small dummy, walking to heel on a lead, then through to dropping, staying dropped and so on to the full treatment outlined in this book.

The really impressionable age is five to twelve months. From twelve months onwards establishment or 'bedding in' is the natural sequence to basic training. At this age and stage of training, solitary kennelling is beneficial. If possible, commence it at five months old, for solitary kennelling will rapidly create a new personality. The new character emerges simply because the pupil has to face its trainer, realities and the world, without the support of its companions. It has to rely entirely on its own devices, its own reactions thereby becoming moulded by habit-forming guidance from its trainer. It is all just as simple as that.

If the daily approach can continue without side effects the perfect dog emerges. Unfortunately, however, clever as you may be, side effects and distractions do develop and create headaches for both pupil and trainer. For instance, the pup may not want to come to its kennel when told, a small, common and apparently insignificant occurrence, but do not be deceived. It can be the beginning of the battle for mastery. If on the very first day your pupil shows signs of reluctance to come, you perceive the line of thinking that is rapidly going to develop into rebellion and you deal with it gently but firmly by shutting an outside door to prevent escape, or place a light lead to guide the pup. You avoid creating a situation that can rapidly deteriorate or develop into a major issue which would destroy all confidence.

It can, of course, be overcome by a method of eatable rewards, used by many but not favoured by me. I expect a dog to do what I tell it without having to give more than a pat of appreciation, or a word of encouragement. It does help, too, to tell the pupil what a wonderful fellow he is, and how much better you like him when he does what he is told. You will be surprised how this is understood and appreciated. Single kennelling also eliminates other distracting interests. I find this most advantageous, in fact the elimination of other interests at all times in training is most helpful and creates the right atmosphere for the pupil to absorb his lessons.

By other attractions I refer to other dogs, hot game scent, or third parties being present. I hate a pup that keeps running off to a watching friend when you yourself are trying to induce it to do something completely different. In fact it can be beneficial to give separate lessons on actually 'giving' attention regardless of the surroundings. This can be done by telling the pup to sit, making it look you directly in the eye, holding its attention eye to eye while you talk to it, not letting its eye wander. Some dogs, like humans, cannot stare you straight in the eye. I like the dog who rivets his eyes and attention on you and you alone when you are addressing it, seriously or otherwise. This is the dog that gives results. Every time it is silently conveying to you 'I love you, I love you, I love you, what do you expect of me, how can I please you?'

When obedience has been established to a point of reasonable control I like to commence the development of natural instincts. This is the most successful and satisfactory form of training, whereby a gradual programme of progressive development allows full play for the inherited instincts (so carefully planned by breeders over the years) to come gradually to the fore. Then the obedience control already taught can be introduced in conjunction, at the time when these instincts are emerging from their living but dormant state.

Pupils should be allowed to solve their own problems, and they should be introduced to game scent with patience and understanding. By that, I mean time to allow the discovery of pleasures to come. They must eat the bread and butter before starting even on the plain cake. The rich cream cakes can come later on, when fuller maturity is approaching, when handling of live game and collecting runners fulfil the ultimate desires. The deferred instincts are then released to be controlled by the foundation training that has already resulted in a controllable pupil.

Deferred instincts may well vary from dog to dog so the development and advancement can only be assessed by assessing each individual. Even style may be latent and will only emerge with fuller knowledge of game scents and complete confidence in the trainer. Range of hunting and the pattern only comes with certainty from constant habit-forming stamping-in. It is much easier to open a dog's hunting range than it is to reduce it, very much easier. Situations can then be manufactured to create simple problems that can be solved by the pupil, such as previously hidden dummies or cold game actually on the hunting beat—take care to try and leave no human foot scent as this soon leads to a puppy tracking foot scent to find game. This must be avoided for it acts as a diversion.

I like to drop a dummy or game on the beat in full sight of the pup, then proceed to walk on, sending the dog back for a retrieve. Increase the distance daily until the dog can return over long distances to collect at the order of the trainer. This may not be an essential in gundog training but it does develop the pupil's intelligence and amenability. The delight shown by the pupil after a long retrieve fully confirms the point. It helps to satisfy the natural instincts by artificial means.

The same procedure can be followed in teaching a pup to jump, cross water or remain steady while another dog retrieves. The latter really does help to eliminate jealousy, which becomes such a danger to a one man, one dog combination. It should always be borne in mind that the situations should be simple at the commencement and become increasingly more severe. It is very important that the dog succeeds. Failures and disappointments should be avoided. The pupil should learn to be a success, should expect to be a success, it will then be a success. Success breeds success. Then you have an attractive dog—a gay dog.

It is important that the showing of displeasure and the infliction of punishment be clear and concise, and absolutely on the scene of the crime. It must be administered with great understanding and tempered with justice. At an early age, a pupil will soon learn the displeasure in your voice. This should suffice for quite a while. Then if persistent disobedience follows, strong measures may be adopted. But never to the extent of breaking the confidence or spirit of the pupil. It should be on the exact spot where disobedience took place. If for chasing sheep, the handler must follow hard on the tail of the chaser and catch him in the act. It is useless to wait for his return before punishing; for you would then be punishing for something you have already taught must be done, i.e. returning to you.

The length of the training period must be determined by the progress of the pupil. I would expect to take a sixteen-week-old pup and have it in reasonable shape by nine months old, and by fifteen months to have it ready for full introduction to shooting conditions. However, there are always exceptions to the rule, and the time varies considerably. The sensible trainer will make no haste to finish a slow developer nor retard a quick progresser. So no fixed time can really be laid down as a yardstick. Each trainer has his own personality and must train to his own temperament. The pupil will then respond accordingly and will develop accordingly, influenced by the facilities the trainer may have, but there is no substitute for perseverance, regularity and hard work.

At this time a marriage can be arranged between obedience and developing instincts, whereby the driving desire to hunt and flush comes under the control of the basic training which has been previously completed. The procedure to consummate the marriage to its fulfilments is portrayed in detail throughout this book. The child of the marriage should be an efficient, co-operative, companionable gun-dog.

Professional Training

There are two avenues of approach when deciding the most important questions of all, who will train my future dog? To what standard and for what purpose? When will it be ready for shooting or field trials? How much will it cost if trained by a professional? Am I capable of tackling the job myself? These are questions that will all have to be answered before a decision can be made.

The first and easiest approach is to hand the youngster to a well-known professional trainer who is thoroughly experienced in these matters. You will inquire about his charges and the time required to finish the job before deciding. Most trainers will take at least twenty-six weeks, so with the ever increasing costs of feed and equipment the expense can be considerable. Sometimes, when training has progressed for a time it becomes obvious the pup is not going to be a success. This causes disappointment, financial loss and a wasted effort, not forgetting a cast-off pup to dispose of. If you keep the puppy on his return from the trainer, loyalties will have been established between trainer and pup which take time to mend after the lapse in ownership. Loyalties will have to be re-established when the dog returns.

As the purpose of this book is to encourage the training of dogs by amateurs my advice is to tackle the job yourself. The resulting fun, adventure and satisfaction will be most rewarding, giving relaxation from the heat and pressures of everyday life. Short periods daily or as often as possible are adequate to achieve reasonable results. It is not necessary to have large areas of land to hunt over, rabbit pens to steady in or game to hunt ad lib. All the basic training can be done around the house on a small lawn or other suitable patch. All the better if more spacious areas are available, for wide open spaces are always pleasant for pupil and trainer although restricted areas are quite adequate for satisfactory results.

The next decision will be the design and siting of the kennel. Try to plan for sufficient freedom of movement so that a delayed homecoming does not unduly worry you or your dog or interfere with your or his daily routine. If self-feeding and watering are installed the dog can be left unattended for several days. Self-feeding must be used with discretion and understanding, or a greedy dog or puppy will soon run to overweight.

(And now, back to Mr. Carlton.)

2

Spaniels for Sport

To a dog's character incessant thrashings are fatal. Under such treatment he becomes either cowed or case-hardened (see pages 44 and 45) according to his individual temperament, but never trained. Doubly true is this if the thrashings are undeserved. *Under just treatment* he will render you the hero-worship of a 'dame's school' boy to his Eton brother; you will be to him the one whom it is his pleasure to serve and to whom he instinctively looks for guidance if he finds himself at fault.

See as much of your dog as you possibly can. Gain his confidence; you will do no good with a dog that is suspicious of you. Give yourself a chance of discovering any outstanding traits in his character and apply the knowledge so gained in your treatment of him—it is rarely that any two dogs can be trained in exactly the same way. Leave no stone unturned to get a good performance at the wind-up of every lesson.

Refrain from continuously nagging at your dog; assume that he desires to please you and in consequence he is wishful of pleasing you and obeying your commands. Do not pick a quarrel with him needlessly, but seek to keep on good terms as long as you possibly can.

Do not expect your training to result in even progress; it is sure to have its ups and downs. One day all will go well, the next nothing goes right. He has his good days and his bad, but so have you. Your mood and his act and re-act on one another. On his bad days blame yourself, get him to perform well some easier task, and take him home.

Just as there are bad days so there are bad places, which your puppy appears to dislike for no apparent reason. Associations are strong. If your puppy has once been especially perverse, avoid the scene of his perverseness and never give him a lesson there again.

Never give a lesson unless you have your puppy's whole attention, or continue one when you have lost it. To do so is to annoy both him and yourself and profit neither. Take every opportunity of getting him interested in the scent of game; you cannot directly teach him to use his nose, but you can, and must, give him opportunities to teach himself.

Take every opportunity of developing his brains. Let him find out things for himself where possible. Let him solve his own problems as much as possible. Do not be impatient if, on his first experience of the road, he jibs at every sight and smells at every passer-by. The world is new to him, and he must get to know it in his own way—mostly by the nose. Have you ever noticed how throughout his life a dog relies on nose? He will pick you out in a crowd by sight, but rarely seems sure that it is you until he has your scent.

For successful training patience is more than a virtue, it is essential.

In many of the older books you are advised to train your puppy by taking him out with a trained dog. In later books this method is decried. The derision has, I think, been overdone. There is a happy medium. To let the example of a trained dog be your sole method is obviously wrong, as likely as not you will find your puppy waiting outside a thick place for the older dog to flush the game. Training by jealousy, especially in retrieving, is, however, bulking large in the eyes of many modern gundog men. It is impossible to lay down any rules for applying it, and I have not dealt with the subject specifically.

Your own 'dog sense' can be your only guide. Perhaps a single instance out of my own experience may be of use. A puppy, nearly finished, was perfect at retrieving rabbits cold, but refused to pick them up when freshly killed. After each refusal I tied him up, went home and brought another dog, and sent this to retrieve. On replacing the rabbit, the culprit each time did all that had been asked before of him in vain. As a finish I used him as a retriever a time or two while another dog was hunting. By these methods, both based on jealousy, his fault was corrected.

When you give a command or signal to your dog, do it with your whole heart. The flabbier your state of mind, the flabbier is your dog's response. The intangible bond between man and dog varies much with different dogs and varies more between different men. A harsh inconsistent trainer can rarely make a cowed or case-hardened dog susceptible to this power of will. I am convinced that a distinct command forms an important element in good training.

Avoid the use of lead and check-cord as far as possible. Your puppy will progress more rapidly without them. Finally, to train a dog properly, a man must always be attentively on the watch to nip crime in the bud; and it is the lack of this ability in would-be trainers that accounts for so many failures, while the possessors of it are succeeding without apparent trouble or even method. I have in the following notes endeavoured to suggest a method; the development of this ability rests with you. Its foundations lie in the interest you take in the progress of your training, and it is built up by observing the rule 'Watch your dog'.

Comments on Chapter 2

A woman, a spaniel and a walnut tree, the more you beat them the better they be, is the old image of a self-willed, uncontrollable, headstrong spaniel common on all estates before and at the turn of the century. Another old story tells of a shooting host saying to the head keeper at the meet, 'After you have beaten the spaniels we will make a start'. This old image has, with some justification, 'stuck', principally because the introduction of drive and speed has been so often mistaken for wildness.

Through the 1920's and 1930's many estates with good gundog kennels concentrated on a breeding policy designed to increase drive, speed and style and at the same time to soften the temperament and increase the intelligence and trainability. Over the years this policy has borne fruit until today it is fatal to rough handle or beat the sensitive intelligent youngsters that now have to be trained for modern conditions which demand a high standard of steadiness.

Case hardening which quickly develops is the most common fault if the pupil is continually nagged and punished on a minor basis for repeatedly disregarding his handler— whereas, one quick sharp lesson of correction should achieve the desired effect. Threatening too should be avoided. Dogs so quickly learn to know when a threat will not be substantiated. Give them an inch and they take a yard. Impatience too can react until the puppy actually waits for an impatient action or command before complying with the original request, and then responds in an uncertain and hasty way which quickly develops into a background of hesitation and uncertainty. (See note on case hardening at the end of this chapter).

The reference to training with an older finished dog is interesting. There is no doubt that it introduces jealousies which can be dangerous to the pupil and the training programme, but these influences can also be introduced to great advantage if used with thought and discretion. For instance, walking to heel can be made easier by coupling a pup to an older dog who has already learned to walk to heel. First lessons in hunting can be considerably assisted by an experienced companion seeking game on an approved pattern, providing no undue pressure has to be exerted to control the older dog. I favour dual training until such a time as the youngster has the full confidence and knowledge to operate singly. The advice to 'watch your dog' is extremely sound, therein lies the heart of contact and reactions. You, yourself, are compelled to concentrate if your whole attention is directed on your dog. The dog knows and appreciates this and will react accordingly.

Dual training is a most entertaining method of developing youngsters from four to seven months. Nothing gives more confidence than outings with a trained dog—of course, great care must be taken with sheep and other livestock because pups very quickly delight in chasing anything that will run. Consequently, great care should be taken to avoid circumstances which include opportunities to chase livestock. If, accidentally a chase takes place immediate action must be taken to convey strong disapproval to the culprit.

I like to select suitable open heath; broken ground, bracken or similar cover is excellent as there is no opportunity to chase and a youngster should continually be looking for you as it becomes lost in the cover. Keep contact with an occasional whistle, change direction from time to time, lifting the youngsters by whistle and directing them to the new ground by making a definite movement yourself—approaching new covert at a quicker pace with a sense of urgency. This conveys control without pressures. It can be developed to great advantage, and provide good fun for the handler, too.

Special Notes on Case Hardening

Continual nagging of a dog or child produces in both a total disregard of requests, commands or orders. In children it creates an atmosphere of non-concern and rebellion, as well as direct refusal to obey the simplest request. In fact, non-compliance becomes a natural sequence to any order given. In the same way continual admonishment and punishment, corporal or otherwise, of a young dog quickly resolves itself into an expected sequence to any command given. It often commences in an unexpected way and like drug-addiction it becomes established without the taker realizing it has happened. Slight punishment is dealt out for a misdemeanour, the following day the same thing happens until the punishment, starting as slight, soon becomes severe until very heavy-handed methods are resorted to to regain control. In the meantime the dog has grown so accustomed to punishment and/or nagging that it no longer has any fear of the admonishment and becomes wilful, even 'Bolshie'. This is what I mean by case hardening. I am sure a pup should not be continually threatened. A command should be given and obedience should be expected. I do like to see and insist that obedience has resulted. However, if open rebellion does appear it can take two forms,

> starting with   (1) Playful rebellion
> developing into   (2) Wilful rebellion.

The first can be passed off with a sense of humour fitting the occasion. The second must be dealt with firmly and resolutely according to the degree of disobedience. Playful rebellion can often develop into wilful rebellion. The age of the youngster must be taken into serious consideration, because it may not have reached the age of discretion when it can be fully responsible for its own reactions to orders given. Therefore, if the pup is young all except the simplest commands should be avoided so as to ensure compliance. If punishment is given for disobedience I like a period of time to elapse, maybe one day, maybe two before that same order is given again, thus allowing the pupil time for thought. The same command should be given in such a way, and at such a time and a place, as will ensure that it will be understood and obeyed. Then and only then, can the order be constantly repeated to establish the command. But do not nag, nag, nag, or you will reap the harvest of disobedience.

(Again, back to Mr. Carlton.)

3

The Perfect Spaniel

'The preliminary course is by far the most important'—it is impossible to repeat this too often. But on what lines should it run? To what is it preliminary?

Before starting to train your spaniel, you must have and keep clearly before you the full picture of what you want him to do when trained.

Everyone who uses a spaniel as a general purpose dog knows that he wants his dog to:

(1) Seek and flush game.
(2) Drop to shot.
(3) Collect on command.

This statement of requirement is in absurdly simple terms. It serves, however, in affording three headings under which to consider the matter in greater detail, viz., hunting, steadiness and retrieving.

1. HUNTING

Method, pace and style: it is not enough that your spaniel should find some game—he should find all the game within easy gunshot on either side of you, hunting with continuity, rhythm and determination—investigating every likely holding place. In the eyes of field trial judges there is no fault—except a hard mouth—that is so unforgivable as passing game, and this fault is, I think, more often due to lack of thoroughness in working the ground than to lack of nose.

The fault that is hardly less—perhaps equally unforgivable —is pottering.

To the man who goes out 'spanielling' for his own amusement, I fancy that pottering annoys him more than passing game—the pottering is a visible source of annoyance all the time, whereas the game his dog has missed might, for all he knows, not be there at all. Personally, and I am not alone in this, I would prefer to shoot over a dog that goes a good pace or speed and misses a rabbit or bird every now and then rather than one that goes at half the pace and finds every one. It is, to my mind, a more artistic and enjoyable performance and, noses being equal, the fast dog's bag will be the larger at the end of the day; he will have covered much more ground.

Whatever views you may hold as to the passing of game, it is undeniable that the two great things to aim at in your training are an effective method of working the ground and pace—so long as pace does not result in the dog over-running his nose.

Style, also, is by no means a negligible quality. It is the outward sign of keenness and game-finding capacity. It may be spoilt by bad training; it may develop from those abilities of which it is the sign, namely keenness and game-finding, but it cannot, I think, be put into a dog that is wholly lacking in it. Some naturally fast puppies are apt, in their early days, to gallop their ground from the mere joy of pace; when steadied down their style improves; their pace becomes subservient to their nose and their handler.

Method of working and pace are matters directly within the control of the trainer, the one absolutely, the other in a minor degree.

A spaniel is often the counterpart of his handler; if the handler is dull and listless, and especially if he takes a somewhat tepid interest in his dog, his dog is slow and apathetic. If the handler is keen and alert to discover the least indication that his dog is on a scent, the dog responds to his handler's interest and hunts the better for him. The method of working is a bigger matter. It must of course depend to a large extent

47

upon the nature of the ground. Nothing need be said here about working a large isolated patch of brambles, gorse or briars, or a hedgerow. A spaniel that will not work the thick is no spaniel at all.

On open ground, such as a rough piece or an expanse of dead bracken or heather, it is no uncommon sight to see a spaniel working out of gunshot. Or, at the other extreme, if there has been some pretence of training, he may trot off listlessly straight in front of the gun, feel that he has got far enough, wait for his handler to come up to him, and then trot on again. He may start a rabbit or two in the course of the day—the gun would probably have kicked up most of them himself. Again, at the limit of his range he may flush a pheasant when the gun would have had a better chance if the flushing had been left to him. In such a case, gun and dog together may have been beating a strip of country not much more than five yards wide. In neither of these cases does the dog add much to the bag; he might almost as well have been left at home or, if a good retriever, have been used solely as such.

To be a really effective aid to sport, the spaniel should be working a strip thirty or forty yards wide (see page 98) with the gun walking up the centre of it and the dog now going out and working to the right, now turning smartly crossing in front of the gun and going out at an equal distance to the left, and so with repetition of the movement quartering his ground. He should not dwell on a rabbit run or other unprofitable scent, but bring every tussock and bush within the range of his nose, pushing through every patch that is not fully commanded from outside—all the time with his tail going merrily and his every action indicating the joy of hunting and a keen desire to get the gun a shot, while making use of wind direction at all times.

I must not be taken to mean that the quartering should be unduly systematic or is all that is required. Mere quartering would reduce the spaniel to the level of a beater. He must be

1. **Warmth of autumn.** The author with F. T. Champion, Saighton's Stinger on a hot October day's shooting round the boundaries, where the pheasant ground meets the moor

2. **Expressions as a key to character.** 1. Alertness and 'life'; 2. The attitude of attention; 3. Intensity; 4. One who looks a man straight in the eye; 5. A good dark eye; 6. Softness, to counterbalance zest and drive. *See page* 35

3. **Humanization is essential.** Cyrilla Lady Belhaven gives two lessons: (*above*) a first retrieve at about ten weeks; (*below*) satisfaction for inborn curiosity at eight weeks. *See page 33*

4. **Four stages in a retrieve.** First (*above*) the find after a hunt in heather; then the pick-up; (*below*) quickly and cleanly done.

(*Above*) A fast, confident come-in, the bird carried lightly but surely: (*below*) a good delivery, the tender hold not relaxed until the bird is safely placed to hand. *See page* 68

5. **Spaniels in the sea.** Fearlessness in water should be characteristic of every gundog. Eight of the Saighton's springers in and out of the waves on an Anglesey shore. *See page* 112

6a. **A lily pool makes an ideal schooling site for water work.** On return the retrieve is carried high and confidently

6b. **Stone wall tactics.** Saighton's Streamline shows how to retrieve an 8-lb. hare across a familiar obstacle in northern Britain. The wall is three feet high.
See page 123

7. **Two angles on jumping.** (*Above*) the camera records a well-collected jump, the obstacle cleared cleanly but with economy. (*Below*) how a dog may have to land, showing the importance of sound conformation to withstand the shock. Stinger again. *See pages* 121-3

using his nose every moment of the time, taking every advantage of the wind and working every likely bit of ground —with half an eye on his handler's whereabouts all the time.

With a spaniel hunting as I suggest he should, it is obvious that pace is greatly to be desired. He has to work—and work thoroughly—to and fro across a strip not less than thirty to forty yards wide, while the gun is walking up the middle of it. If the dog is slow, time will be wasted, or possibly the gun may get impatient, hurry the dog, and make him miss much ground. In either case the bag suffers; and the best dog is the dog that best fills the bag.

In connection with pointers and setters, it has frequently been stated that pace and nose are by no means canine opposites; with spaniels, this is equally true. Pace as a rule is associated with keenness, and for this reason the fast dog is more likely to be using his nose than a slower one. The keener the dog, the more likely he is to bring into play every game-finding attribute he has; of these he is well aware that his nose is the best and most reliable.

Comments on Chapter 3

The perfect dog has yet to appear. Breeders strive to breed the unbeatable, anticipating that the next litter will produce the perfect specimen. We have all had our favourites, we have all had outstanding workers, but only a very courageous person would say he'd produced the perfect spaniel.

I have seen some wonderful workers during the last thirty years and many notable performances. The outstanding feat in my experience was the retrieving of a wing tipped goose which fell on sticky soft mud at Frampton-on-Severn. Several strong Labradors made the attempt but failed and returned empty-handed. Finally Sam, an old Field Trial dog of mine in his twelfth year, with tremendous guts and drive, was called. He struggled to the fall through mud up to his belly. Then he took off after the goose which he eventually collected, and the tremendous effort to return commenced across nearly half a mile of soft holding mud, but now with the added weight of the wing-tipped front. Resting frequently to regain breath and strength he eventually proudly arrived and presented the bird to his thrilled owner. A very experienced shooting party all agreed that it was one of the most courageous feats they had ever seen a dog undertake. Many spectacular collections of runners over long distances are remembered in photographic clearness because the skill, determination and speed needed over hill or across dale make such an indelible impression, particularly when every false move is quickly corrected until the final drive into the wounded bird perhaps a mile away.

One cold windy morning on the coast my dog Spree had marked a mallard drake down five yards from the shore. I sent him immediately to collect but the duck, only wounded, had already started to swim strongly out to sea assisted by a strong off-shore wind. Before it had gone far its broken wing, caught by the wind, rose like a sail lending more sailing power to the already quick moving duck. When the dog started to swim it was within two yards of the duck but, with the help of the wing acting as a sail, the mallard was able to swim at exactly the same speed as the dog. Both animal and bird continued to swim out to sea, maintaining the same dividing distance. The strong off-shore wind gave a sense of false security to the spaniel who had not thought of the well-nigh impossible task of returning. He continued swimming, encouraged by the close proximity of the duck, until 500 or 600 yards out to sea. His keenness swept aside all thought of defeat, so the battle continued into larger waves until both were out of sight. What eventually happened I never knew, but I had already said good-bye to one of my favourites, and a Field Trial Champion at that. After a considerable lapse of time when I had given up all hope, I suddenly saw a speck, which was my spaniel's head battling back against wind and waves. Fortunately he had no duck—otherwise I know he would never have made it. He would have been doomed, because I am positive he would never have released that duck once he had retrieved. The extra weight would have beaten him. I whistled encouragement until he eventually landed in an exhausted condition. This was the nearest I have ever been to losing a dog wildfowling.

There are many examples of such prowess, which illustrate the drive a good spaniel must have. Field Trial Champion Spurt O'Vara once forcibly broke the ice to collect a dead pheasant away on a frozen lake, returning via the same channel. Probably the gamest action of any spaniel was that of a bitch wildfowling with me on an inland sea. It was during the great freeze-up and the sea was actually frozen with a three-inch crust of soft ice. We were waiting on a bridge for flighting duck. At low tide, the parapet was 18 ft. from the water's level. Waiting on the road, I shot a tufted duck which fell over the bridge into the sea. The bitch without hesitation jumped on to the parapet, then down into the sea. Fortunately, the ice was soft enough not to hurt. She forced her way through the slushy ice, collected the duck and swam round to land. This was one of the greatest and most spontaneous retrieves I have ever witnessed.

It would be a brave man who would say any of these dogs were perfect spaniels, although they were outstanding workers. Perhaps the nearest to perfection is a bitch called Lucy who had that wonderful asset, an impeccable temperament—she never wanted to do wrong, totally disregarded ground game when working pheasants, sat unperturbed at the heaviest stand, observed all and patiently waited orders to collect while still remembering most of the falls. She would face any cover and never gave her owner the least concern at the hottest corner. I rate her nearest to perfection. She was not particularly fast, never outstandingly brilliant but just plain honestly consistent. Without orders, fuss or handling she did an efficient job under very exacting conditions. A good looker, typically springer, she would work for any member of the family. All these dogs had two things in common, they had guts and determination; they were all sensitive as youngsters which indicates that sensitivity, sympathetically understood in youth, grows into a great willingness to please at maturity. Combine guts with sensitivity and you have wonderful material to train creatively.

Style is to me the quintessence of the spaniel in action—it is portrayed by a dog full of joie-de-vivre, energetic, attentive, bold, fast-moving, with continuous tail and body action giving the impression that the tail hits the ribs every time it wags. It is obvious to the handler as he watches for the dog receiving 'the message' of interesting scents which absorbs its whole attention while the tail will usually spell out the message: pheasants cock or hen, ground game, or other not so interesting scents. Pottering, so conclusively condemned, is rightly relegated to the older spaniel and the much older gun, for with it the essential excitement is lacking. Pottering is conspicuous by its absence in the modern working spaniel for modern breeding policy has been dominated by the desire to produce fast stylish workers.

(Back to Mr. Carlton.)

4

Basic Requirements

Standing Rabbits

Suppose your spaniel is working in the open and finds a rabbit in its seat. What is he to do? Most spaniel men are agreed that he should not catch it, and that if he does, he should either drop it on command or bring it to hand.

Should the dog poke the rabbit up at once or should he set ('stand') it? If he finds well within gunshot, it does not matter which he does. It is possible, however, that when at the limit of his proper range, especially on a cross wind, he may have got the scent of the rabbit some distance off. If he pokes it up at once the shot will be lost, whereas if he stands to it the gun will have time to get in position. One can hardly expect the average spaniel to make fine distinctions as to distance, especially when he is drawing up on a scent. It is therefore better to teach him, if you can, to stand his rabbits at all times and to start them only when the gun comes up or on command.

I do not mean that he should advance like a pointer or setter or that he should stand indefinitely. As to the two extremes, I think it better that he should dash in and poke the rabbit up at once than stand it too long. The latter not only wastes time but is apt to develop into standing empty seats, in other words 'false pointing'.

It will be noted that the above remarks as to standing rabbits are confined to open ground, and English conditions. If a spaniel is working thick cover, such as gorse, he should at once put up everything he finds and hustle it until it breaks cover and gives the gun a shot. It is wonderful how adept a good dog gets at flushing out rabbits to the gun and dropping, even without a shot being fired, as soon as he sees that they are well away in the open.

Stamina and Perseverance

Your spaniel should be able to keep going all day at his best pace, a matter of stamina, courage and condition; he should also keep on hunting, though he finds no game. Both these qualities are of great importance on most rough shoots, and it is to be deplored that they can rarely be tested at field trials—the one for lack of time, the other because there must be a quantity of game if many spaniels are to have a trial in the course of a short winter's day.

Steadiness

The only degree of steadiness that is essential is such as will ensure that the dog does not spoil the shot and will not, by retrieving without orders, put up other game out of shot or while the gun is unloaded. The best way to achieve this is to train your dog to drop to the flush of game and also drop to shot.

It is, of course, equally good if the dog, instead of dropping, halts. Dropping is, however, the more easily learned for it is a much more definite action. A dropped dog has to get up before he runs-in (breaks), not so one that merely halts, and so is one degree further removed from unsteadiness. It is better that the dropping should take the form of the dog sitting on his haunches rather than lying at full length. Although the latter position is yet another degree removed from running-in (breaking) it prevents 'marking' a 'must' in all dogs that retrieve quickly.

Many seasoned dogs when working in cover over which they cannot see when sitting acquire the habit of standing up on their hind legs to get a better view. This is undoubtedly the best position of all, but I have never heard of any spaniel being directly taught to do this. It comes from keenness and is not taught, although I see no reason why it should not be, if life were long enough. I find it is noticeably hereditary.

In connection with steadiness, as with hunting, there are two matters for which a spaniel is not usually tried at field trials. The one is walking to heel; the other is steadiness in a grouse butt or at a partridge drive or covert shoot. Despite this no spaniel can be called perfect unless he can do both these as well as being a no-slip retriever, and also able to sit without whining.

Retrieving

Your spaniel having dropped to fur or wing should not, of course, retrieve without orders. He should not even start forward at the shot. He should be rock steady. In the case, too, of fur or feather which he has not found or even seen, he should be trained to drop instantly to shot at whatever pace he may be going. Having dropped, he should not move until he is sent out to retrieve or has the command to go on hunting, the usual word for which is 'gone away' or 'seek on'.

With regard to retrieving fur or feather which your spaniel has not found, a spaniel's duties do not differ from a retriever's. When, however, it comes to retrieving fur which he has found, a complication arises.

Suppose a rabbit which your spaniel has started from its seat goes twenty yards all the time out of his sight, and is then shot and legged and crawls on another thirty yards. Your spaniel should get on the line at or just beyond the seat and take it right up to the rabbit. This line for its first twenty yards is a live foot-scent, and it is only for the last thirty yards that it is what is generally termed a blood-scent. When your spaniel is hunting he should not, as pointed out in the first section of this chapter, take any notice of a live foot-scent unless his nose tells him that the rabbit is just ahead of him, or at the most should just acknowledge it and leave it. The dog should go straight to the fall or, in the case of ground game, to the exact spot where the shot struck the ground. The powder scent is soon established. Blood-scent will be recognized immediately by an intelligent dog and the line taken to the retrieve.

A retriever is trained to disregard a live scent at all times and under all circumstances. He is kept to heel unless the game is down. Not so the poor spaniel. He finds a rabbit in its seat, starts it, sees it no more, but hears the shot; if the rabbit is hit, he will be expected, on receiving the appropriate command, to take the line from seat to rabbit; if it is missed he must be prepared, on receiving the 'Gone away', to ignore the same line absolutely and go on hunting as if it did not exist.

To unravel these complications in your spaniel's mind takes more time than any of the spectators, possibly even some of the judges, at field trials can appreciate, unless they are themselves trainers. The safest method is to train your spaniel to disregard foot-scents at all times except when he receives some such command as 'Fetch it'. As a rule, and especially at field trials where the rabbits may have been stunk out for weeks and are possibly on the move all day, there will be many live foot-scents that your spaniel should ignore to each one he should take. Let ignoring them be the rule; let taking them, which is the exception, be the subject of a special word of command.

Comments on Chapter 4

Since the disappearance of the rabbit it is even more important to teach your dog to find game birds by body scent alone. To add to the complications of a spaniel's life, all that is expected of a retriever is expected of a spaniel. He should 'mark' well, cast himself, work to hand if necessary, take the wind, be fast and sure on a line, pick up smartly, be tender mouthed, return at the gallop, and deliver well. In addition, he does all the other things a retriever is not usually asked to do.

Once upon a time my life centred around the rabbit even to the extent of a maintained warren surrounded by a five foot wall. In 1950, 19,600 trapped rabbits were sold off the estate, and in addition a further 2,000 were shot over the spaniels. Under these circumstances training spaniels was a great joy and the whole procedure of training simplified. Similar conditions prevailed over the whole of the British Isles, trial grounds were easily obtainable and experienced shots made the competition keen and exciting. But with one fell swoop myxomatosis swept the countryside and rabbits for the time being were no more. Pockets began to reappear only to be wiped out again. Sometimes the disease now reappears and gives the impression that immunity is increasing. However, under these circumstances rabbits for sport are a thing of the past and a reassessment of training has taken place. After a difficult time of re-establishment, working spaniels which adapt themselves to game only have become accepted. There is no doubt that in the absence of the rabbits, hares have considerably increased and so our spaniels still have to be taught to be steady to moving fur. A large hare makes a formidable retrieve for a small spaniel so I believe the emphasis in the future will be on larger spaniels which specialize in handling birds and hares only. The old unwanted reference to 'rabbiting dogs' is now a thing of the past.

The question of pointing or standing game is entirely a matter of personal preference. The Americans, with justi-fication, hate it, because their trial rules insist that the ap-proach to game and the flush must be firm and definite. Therefore any hesitation on the approach severely penalizes them in competition. In this country the trial judges do not penalize until the 'point' is held long enough to become annoying and embarrassing. Since the disappearance of the rabbit I have rather amended my views and now I like a dog to go boldly into the flush because I find it so much more exciting. As most standing or pointing in spaniels is man-made during training, it is comparatively easily introduced into early training, especially if a rabbit pen is available. If continual encouragement to hold the approach is given this is soon established and pointing or standing quickly develops.

Stamina and perseverance are extremely important in the make-up of the general character of the spaniel. The desire to drive on regardless is one of the most important attributes to consider in a breeding policy. A fit and well, second-season spaniel will travel great distances during a hard day's work. I have tried to convert a long day into actual mileage. It is estimated that a pack of hounds sometimes covers eighty miles in the day. I consider that a spaniel covers at least fifty miles and in addition has the arduous task of hustling and bustling through thick cover. The will, bodily structure and physical fitness must all be in tune to allow it to undertake this enormous task and a few days' rest between big days is advantageous.

Steadiness, too, is another important attribute to consider in the breeding policy. Great strides have been taken in breeding out the wilful, unsteady brute which was a legacy of the past. Now a steady spaniel is expected and accepted as a normal gundog and if the training instructions contained in this book are closely followed not much difficulty should be experienced in producing a really steady dog. I would especially emphasize that it is vital to refrain from continuous retrieves, either in training or under actual shooting conditions; nothing 'undoes' a young dog quicker than retrieving every time a shot is fired or a dummy is thrown in training. Great discretion must be exercised for at least the first half of the first season. It is advisable to take pleasure in watching your dog sit under control while another retrieves. Confining it to one retrieve out of four or five birds shot will soon establish in a sensible dog's mind that it must wait for instructions before dashing off to collect. From the foregoing it will be observed that there is a very close relationship between establishing steadiness and retrieving, so the instructions outlined in this chapter must be followed very intelligently.

Blood-scents do take time to learn and consequently only experience teaches a dog to know when he is hunting a cripple and that he must persevere regardless until he collects, and that he must stick to the line through thick and thin and must learn to disregard all foot-scents other than a cripple's. This is facilitated by the dog hunting for body-scent with his nose off the ground instead of pottering and exploring foot-scents. Urging and encouragement must be given to the dog who is puzzling and pottering on the cold scents of unshot birds, but not to the extent of upsetting his concentration.

I attach great importance to marking. Some dogs do mark better than others for this great asset runs in families and some dogs are assisted by better eyesight. Marking is one of the easiest things to teach a spaniel and should present no great difficulties.

(Back to Mr. Carlton.)

PART TWO

Handtraining

5

Handtraining

Early Puppyhood Lessons—Humanization

In most books on dog training, the reader is advised to spend his time during the early months of the puppy's life, say for the first four months after weaning, in making the puppy 'generally' obedient. This is the humanization period.

There is no doubt that this is excellent advice. The difficulty is to know on what lines the trainer should proceed and the nature of the lessons best adapted to secure general obedience. You should no doubt teach the puppy his name, which may be done by calling his name and patting him or giving him a piece of biscuit. You should also, no doubt, make the puppy gallop up to you on his name being called which may be done in much the same way. In addition, you should make him go to his kennel when desired. This presents more difficulty. If a puppy is disobedient in this respect I generally get him to me and either pick him up and carry him or put him on a short light cord, and make him comply by a mixture of cajolery and gentle force ending up with a reward.

In these lessons, as with all other lessons during early puppyhood, the four cardinal principles are:

(1) Never give an order without seeing that the puppy complies with it. He has got to learn to obey you always, not sometimes.

(2) Always be absolutely gentle, both in voice and action. When you come to work in the field, you want a bold keen dog, not a cowed and listless wreck.

(3) Never give an order to which you cannot secure instant compliance without a display of harshness.

(4) Never persist in any lesson which is becoming a bore to the puppy, i.e. continual retrieves of a dummy.

The nearer these earliest lessons can be made to seem like a game in the puppy's eyes, the better. The early stages should be carried out in an atmosphere of playfulness.

Try by encouragement to teach the puppy to solve its own problems; for example set puzzles for it. Within the limits laid down above, the ingenious trainer may teach these lessons in any way that occurs to him, or give such other lessons with the object of inculcating general obedience as his ingenuity may suggest.

Why, in these early days, should one confine one's lessons to securing general obedience? Why not at the same time begin teaching and securing obedience in some of the items which you will eventually have to teach your dog? In the last chapter, a spaniel's work has been considered under the three headings of hunting, steadiness and retrieving. Although this is the natural order in which spaniels' duties are performed it is not the order in which his preliminary education should begin. A spaniel's first lessons should, as a rule be taken in a different order, i.e. hunting, retrieving and lastly steadiness.

This change in order is particularly important in the case of a puppy under six months old. Retrieving can be started 'in suitable surroundings' at twelve weeks old and should continue daily—but no more than two or three retrieves should be given at each lesson with no more than two lessons daily. I do not mean that you should keep your puppies carefully secluded in kennel or run at such times as they are not being given definite lessons. Give them as much liberty and see as much of them as you can. They must get to know their world and learn to put implicit confidence in you. Seize every opportunity of getting scent into their noses. Personally, as soon as my puppies can walk I spend many an odd few minutes with them among the game scents and watch for the first indication of their taking up a scent. Avoid, however, places where the dogs, later on, are likely to get a 'view' and chase. Take care also that they do not acquire too great a liking for hare or rabbit runs. In both cases prevention is better than cure.

One of the methods of teaching retrieving (other methods are mentioned in Chapter 4) is to throw something for the dog to fetch and, without the use of a check-cord or other artificial aid, induce the dog to bring the object up to you. This method can be more successfully employed when the dog is well under the age of six months than at any later age. A puppy must not be allowed to play with the dummy. When a puppy tends to carry the retrieve off in another direction, a passage of wire-netting (narrow) is a suitable place for the return to hand. In the absence of a passage, a light check-cord can be used.

The other lesson which can be successfully taught during these early days is dropping to command, and to hand, which is extended to fur, feather and shot, as the reader will again be reminded in later pages. This is the foundation of steadiness. A puppy can also be taught to sit and hold a dummy in its mouth. This ensures a perfect delivery later on. A word of warning again—never bore the puppy by over-doing the lessons.

This 'dropping' is not only valuable as being one of the things that your dog will eventually have to learn. It also has a value peculiar to itself in inculcating general obedience and making the dog feel himself subservient to his master. It is, in fact, of the very essence of all good spaniel training. A spaniel that will drop instantly to command or hand, wherever he may be and at whatever pace he may be going, has proceeded further in his training and approached more nearly to the completely trained dog than the performance of such an apparently simple action would lead the novice to believe. The drop must be happy and willing. Reluctant or 'sulky' dropping should be avoided at all costs.

But I can hear some of my shooting friends mutter the ominous word 'over-training' and can also hear some of them advocate letting your puppy run wild and chase, if opportunity offers, up to the age of as much as twelve months. If the would-be trainer is hasty in temper, impatient and harsh of tongue, I should advise him to give heed to their muttering and postpone the dropping lessons until a later age or better still, give up all idea of trying to train the puppy himself. If, however, he takes to heart and carries out in their entirety the general principles laid down above, and in particular that as to gentleness, he need have no fear. His puppy will be as keen and full of dash at the end of these earliest lessons as the puppy that has run riot during this period. Indeed, it is more than likely that if the riotous puppy is at all a nervous one, the sudden check he will have to receive may be a break in his spirit and should be avoided.

The younger the dog the more plastic is his mind and the fewer are the bad habits which he will have contracted and which the trainer may have to cast out. Bad habits are to be avoided like the plague.

Retrieving

When your puppy is weaned and as soon as you feel that by judicious gifts of biscuits from your hand and other strata-gems you have gained his confidence, take your heart in your hand and begin your lessons in retrieving. Be sure, however, that your puppy's confidence in you is thoroughly established. This is vital throughout training. It is not enough that he should not fight shy of you. He must be eager to get to you whenever you appear in sight. It is unreasonable to expect him to bring to you what you have thrown for him to fetch, if he will not race up to you normally without this counter-attraction in his mouth. With these retrieving lessons in mind, it is useful to get him to associate some signal such as clapping your hands while he races back or up to you.

The first actual lesson in retrieving is for you an anxious

moment. If your puppy resolutely refuses to pick up what you have thrown for him, your lessons so far as retrieving is concerned will have to be postponed until a later day in his career, and you will have lost much of the pleasure that is derived from the awakening and improvement of his faculties and the development of the personal bond between yourself and him.

Two questions naturally arise. What are you to throw for him to fetch and where are you to throw it? Whatever you throw should be thrown on grass and not on gravel or anything else that is likely to hurt his nose or mouth or otherwise be unpleasant to him. So long as the puppy can see on the ground the thing you throw, a grass field is better than a close-shaven lawn for it is somewhat easier for the puppy to pick up from it. A writer of authority on the training of retrievers advocates taking the puppy some fields away from home. I think this is sometimes good advice, but personally have not found it necessary to go farther away than the paddock adjoining the puppy's usual run, for at the kennel door is an ideal place to stand as the puppy will make a bee-line back to its nest. The trainer should intercept and take delivery of the dummy in the doorway. Keep this habit up daily until the puppy is confidently retrieving to hand.

Wherever the first lesson is given, it must be in a place that is not the puppy's usual playground. It also must be a place that is free from scent of rabbits or game which may prove too strong a counter-attraction, and a place where there are no distracting influences such as other dogs, people, cattle, horses, sheep or noise of traffic. This sounds like making a mountain out of a molehill and in itself a little thing; but dog-training is a conglomeration of little things and it is of the utmost importance to make a good start at this time. In addition it is also helpful at this stage to get the puppy used to a light lead.

Whichever spot you fix upon, go there alone with your puppy and make much of him. By and by take your pocket-handkerchief, knot and re-knot it into a ball so that there are no loose ends. Get your puppy's interest in it aroused, seize a moment when the puppy is following your hand and hand-kerchief in a forward direction, then throw the handkerchief —of course underhand and in continuation of the movement the puppy is following to a distance of a yard or two. At the same time tell the puppy to 'fetch' it. The puppy sees the handkerchief go as it were, 'follows your hand' and gallops out after it and, we hope, picks it up. If you now act as you have acted before, the puppy is almost sure, for the first few lessons at any rate, to face up to you with the handkerchief just as he had done before without it. Whenever he hesitates, run away from him and he will probably follow. If he starts towards you but is shy of coming right up, try the effect of sitting down. Be careful to avoid any sudden movement, or snatching at the handkerchief. This will make the puppy either sheer away from you or drop the dummy. Your aim is to get the object straight from the puppy's mouth into your hand. If by chance the puppy should be disinclined to give up the object, you must not of course engage in a tug-of-war with him but must gently open his mouth—if necessary even put your hand in and take the object from him. Whatever happens, a hard mouth must be avoided and a tug-of-war is just the thing to give him one. Pressure on the dog's pad by the trainer's toe will always make the dog execute a quick release. But this must not be done until the youngster is at least six months old.

Whether it is better to reward the puppy with a piece of biscuit or other dainty, or simply make a fuss of him, is a moot point. In these early days a reward that appeals to his appetite is the more acceptable and makes the puppy keener to come back to you. On the other hand, if the reward is given every time, the puppy is apt to get into the habit of dropping the object in expectation of the reward, a habit that is most difficult to counteract and one which will cause you infinite trouble in the future. A middle course is probably the safer. Give such a reward the first two or three times, gradually cease doing so, and then reserve it for such times as the puppy begins to show disinclination to return to you, for such moments are sure to arrive.

If the spot you fix on for these first lessons is near the puppy's kennel, make a point of throwing the handkerchief away from the kennel. Stand in the doorway and intercept him on his way back to the kennel. The puppy's inclination is as a rule to take his prize to, and not away from, his kennel. You can make use of this inclination for your own purpose. It is encouragement and not forcefulness in these early lessons that will win the day and with it, your puppy's heart and confidence.

If, by chance, when you have thrown the handkerchief the puppy does not go after it, but still has his attention attracted by your hand, do not try to make the puppy pick it up, but go and pick it up yourself. Come back to the place from which you threw it and try again, making sure the pup sees you throw the object. The reason the puppy did not go out is probably because he did not see the handkerchief leave your hand. In these first lessons, to take the puppy up to the handkerchief and try to make him pick it up is only looking for trouble. What you are to do if the puppy goes out but does not pick up the handkerchief will be dealt with shortly.

As to the nature of the edible reward, anything that the puppy likes and that is easily and cleanly carried in the pocket will do. If ever, during his later lessons, he seems inclined to snatch at the reward, close your hand over it. Say 'gently', and do not let him have it until he has got his eagerness under some measure of control. His proper understanding of 'gently' will be of great use to you in the future if he ever displays a tendency towards roughness in his retrieving work.

The use of the knotted handkerchief in these earliest lessons is a time-honoured institution. It is always handy, is soft, and easily attracts the puppy's attention. Also, it may be that it is of value as being an intimate belonging of the trainer and thus help to lay the foundation of the personal bond between him and his dog. Apart from this, anything soft and conspicuous will do.

If the puppy goes out after your handkerchief and refuses to pick it up, do not bother him further that day. Ring the changes: for example change the training area and change the object thrown, e.g. rolled up rabbit skin, hat, pad, tobacco pouch, glove stuffed with corks etc. Do not risk more than one failure in any one day unless you have discovered some location and object with which you have already achieved success. If you have exhausted your resources put off the puppy's retrieving education until such time as he is old enough for you to apply one or other of the methods indicated in Chapter 4. If you succeed in discovering a location and object which have shown promise of success continue in the same way as if success had crowned your first attempts. Then vary the location.

Be careful not to overdo these retrieving lessons, or the puppy will cease to take an interest in them. Once a day, or at the most twice a day—the second time after a good interval—is quite enough.

As the puppy grows, substitute for the knotted handkerchief other objects of gradually increased bulk and weight e.g. a roll of house flannel or other similar material about a foot long. Gradually enlarge its bulk and weight with a small sand bag, finishing up the handtraining with a roll made up to about the weight of a three-quarters-grown rabbit, with a rabbit skin tied tightly over it with string in such a way as to leave no loose edges.

You have been advised to begin these lessons by throwing the object so that the puppy can see it on the ground. At as early a date as possible in the puppy's education begin to throw the object into places where the puppy has to use his nose to find it, but where it is not too difficult for him to pick it up; i.e. rough grass, a hay field, or light bracken, avoid failures.

A most useful variation, possibly a substitute for all but the very first of these lessons, is to get the puppy to come upon the object without his having seen you throw it at all. Walk with your puppy down wind, seize an opportunity when he is not looking and drop or throw the object. After walking on a score of yards or so, turn round, walk up wind towards the object and encourage the puppy to hunt. It is the natural instinct of the spaniel to seek. This instinct must be allowed to develop over a period of time. If he has a nose and has had sufficient acquaintance with the object to recognize its scent, he should draw up to it from several yards. As soon as he has hold of the object, act in the same way as you were advised to do when the puppy had seen the object thrown.

As soon as your continued use of the 'fetch it' has led your puppy to connect the command with going out to retrieve, you should begin to teach him the command which you intend to use when sending him out to find something he has not seen fall—this is usually 'hie lost'. A judicious mingling of the known command 'fetch it' with the one you are teaching him, coupled with your gradually working him up to the object he has not seen leave your hand, with repeated re-iteration of the new command, will soon teach him its meaning. It should not be long before a single 'hie lost' will send your puppy out seeking for the object with all his soul, but at first let the lesson be an easy one. In practice, the fewer words of command the better. A noisy handler is a menace.

By this time the puppy should be quite proficient at bringing the dummy right up and delivering it to hand without your being under the necessity of moving or running away from him. Be careful, however, about facing the puppy as he comes in. If he shows any inclination to drop the dummy before it reaches your hand, keep your back turned to him and do not take it until he has got well up to, or even just past you. Be careful, also, always to take the dummy from underneath his jaws, pressing it upwards and towards his

71

mouth. If you take it from above or snatch it from him, he will be apt to hang his head and put the bundle down—a fault that you must endeavour at all costs to avoid.

Dropping to Command and Hand

So far, I have said nothing about dropping to command or hand but this must not be taken to mean that lessons in this should be postponed until the handtraining in retrieving is finished or even nearing its end. It is perhaps advisable to postpone such lessons until the end of the first month or so of the retrieving lessons, but no good purpose will be served by putting them off longer.

There will be numerous occasions on which you will be going to have a look at your puppies in their enclosure. On these occasions take with you your usual 'reward' and have the puppies out one at a time. Seize a favourable opportunity, gently press down the puppy's hindquarters with one hand and at the same time give him your reward with the other. This should be accompanied by the command that you intend to use in future to drop your dog.

Most spaniel handlers when their dog is hunting, drop him by the word 'up', generally and more easily pronounced 'hup'. The word is sharp and decisive and, unless the trainer has a strong preference for some other, might as well be used. As you press down the hindquarters and give the reward, say 'hup'. Do not at first try to prevent the puppy from getting up as soon as he likes. All you are aiming for at the moment is to connect the 'up' with dropping, and the dropping with the gift of the reward. This will be the more easily accomplished if, after you have given the first lesson, you never give your puppy anything edible from your hand unless he is in the position of the drop.

In giving the first lessons to very young puppies, you will find your task easier if you sit down on the ground and make the puppy drop by your side.

After the first few lessons make your puppy wait in the

seated position a second or two for the reward. If necessary hold him down with your hand and gradually increase the period of waiting and utilize the delay in holding up your disengaged hand. Carry this further by keeping the puppy dropped still longer, gradually increasing the time you keep him dropped after having given him his reward. Do not let him get up until you have given him the appropriate order.

As to what this should be, you will of course bear in mind the future work of your puppy in the field. In actual work, he will have dropped either to fur, feather, or shot. If he is wanted to retrieve, you have already taught or are in the course of so doing, the appropriate command. When perhaps he is not wanted to retrieve, he will have to go on hunting and the command usually employed is 'gone away'. This command, then, you had better use when allowing your puppy to leave his drop.

So far you have always kept near your puppy and have not attempted to keep him down long. As soon as the puppy drops readily to the combined influence of your 'up' and raised hand, back a foot or two from him with hand raised. Before giving the reward, if he attempts to get up and ignores your 'up', go back to him and put him down again. Gradually increase the distance you back from him, gradually omitting the upraised hand and reserving it for such times as he attempts to get up—every now and then turning your back on him.

The age of the puppy when this period of training is taking place, should be at least five months or preferably seven months. In special cases it can be rewarding to teach an individual puppy these things from sixteen weeks of age onwards. He must stay dropped exactly where you put him until you come back to him. If he gets up while you are away from him, go back and put him down in the exact place at which he ought to have stayed and retreat to at least your original distance before you come back to praise him. Insistence on this exactness will save you great trouble in the future. The puppy will soon understand that, until he does exactly as you desire, he does not get his praise. Sometimes a reward is permissible.

So far, the puppy has only dropped at your side. As soon as he does this readily and stays where he is put until he has received praise, you must one day catch his eye when he is a yard or so away from you and hold up your hand; fortifying this if necessary with your 'up', if he drops. Do not at first keep him waiting long but go up to him and praise him. If he does not drop you must gently force him to in the exact place in which he ought to have done so. If necessary, gently take him to the exact spot, make him drop there, retreat again, and keep him waiting. He will soon tumble to the fact that the more readily he drops, the sooner he will get his praise or reward.

As the puppy gets proficient at dropping a yard or so from you, gradually increase the distance until he finally drops readily and smartly to hand or command however far from you he may be. In all these lessons be careful to proceed slowly. Insist on exact compliance with an order. Increase the difficulty of the lessons gradually and if you feel that you are going too fast for the puppy do not hesitate to go back to easier lessons. Above all things, do not worry your puppy by doing too much at a time.

The great secret of making your puppy steady at his drop is never in these early lessons to call or whistle him up to you from his drop. Always go back to him and give praise before you release him.

Dropping to Fur and Feather

If you are fortunate enough to have an enclosure containing a few rabbits or Belgian hares, or even have a tame rabbit which you can let out of its hutch on to a grass field, you can carry these lessons of early puppyhood still further.

Your lessons in dropping to command and hand have not been so much an object in themselves as the stepping stones

74

to general steadiness in the field, of which the principal element is dropping to fur or feather.

Assuming that you have a pen or have let out your tame rabbit, go fetch your puppy and put him on a light but strong cord two or three yards long. You will previously have accustomed him to some such restraint. Lead the puppy quietly up to within a yard or two of the rabbit, which will probably be feeding in the open, and make him stand there. If he shows any inclination to have a go at it, check him gently but firmly with the cord.

As soon as the rabbit moves, and if it is very tame you will probably have to poke it up with a stick or your foot, drop the puppy with your usual 'up' and in case of need, press down his hindquarters with your hand. Go away from the puppy as far as the length of the cord which you will still hold in your hand. If he attempts to get up before you give him the command, drop him again in the exact spot that he has left.

In course of time, you can leave the puppy dropped. Walk away from him without holding the cord and work the rabbit gradually nearer to him, always taking care that he is not allowed to get up until you come right back to him and give him the command. The only object of these lessons is to teach the puppy to drop to fur, i.e. convert his natural inclination to chase into the drop movement and to ensure he remains dropped in the face of temptation.

As soon as these objects are attained, such lessons should be given very sparingly and only often enough to prevent the puppy from losing the habit he has learnt—and giving play to his natural inclination. Tame rabbits and Belgian hares rarely make seats, and to persevere too far with lessons on them is to encourage your puppy to hunt with his eyes and not, as he should of course do, with his nose. Therefore, never overdo this particular lesson.

If, however, your enclosure also contains wild rabbits, you can carry these early lessons still further. In fact, you can make him hunt in the enclosure just as if he were hunting in the field. Whenever he finds one of the tame variety, he will stand it as usual and drop as it goes away. Leave him dropped a minute or two and then give him the command 'gone away' and start him hunting in a direction opposite to that which the tame rabbit has taken. He will soon come to understand that when a rabbit has been started and the command given, he is to have no more concern with that rabbit, and that he should go on hunting without paying any attention to the rabbit he has started or other rabbits that he may see in the enclosures. The same applies to game flush. By continual flushing with no retrieves, you will ensure that your pupil's correct reactions will become automatic, and he will make no attempt to chase after flushing.

However steady your puppy may be in this enclosure, do not fall into the error of thinking that he is a trained dog. When you hunt him outside you will probably find that sooner or later he relapses into chasing on sight. You have, however, taught him by this enclosure work what he ought to have done, and will have little difficulty in getting him to understand that what he has been accustomed to do in the enclosure, he must also do in the field. Although you have not yet given him any but the most rudimentary lessons in working his ground, you have taught him the difference between right and wrong.

Waiting for Orders before Retrieving

In the retrieving lessons advocated in the earlier part of this chapter nothing has been said about making your puppy wait until he has been told to go out to retrieve.

As soon as he goes out readily, picks up smartly, and returns to you at the gallop, you must begin this part of his education.

In some books on retriever training, you are advised at this stage to put a check-cord on your puppy. You are told to hold or put your foot firmly on the loose end of the cord, throw the dummy or other object as usual, and when the puppy goes out to retrieve, let him be pulled up, probably 'turned turtle', as soon as he gets to the limit of the check-cord. This has always seemed to me a somewhat barbarous and illogical proceeding, and one calculated to dampen most effectually the puppy's eagerness to retrieve. However this may be, it is not in my opinion the way to treat a very young puppy. Better postpone this part of the puppy's education until he will drop and stay where you have put him fairly consistently. In the meantime, do not do too much of the going-out-to-retrieve-without-orders business. You do not want this to become too deep-seated a habit.

When the puppy is fairly good at dropping and staying, drop him by your side and go out a yard or two in front of him keeping your eye on him all the time. If he behaves correctly and shows no inclination to leave his drop, throw the dummy in a direction away from the puppy while raising the other hand; if he attempts to move give him your usual 'up'. You could alternatively come back to your puppy, give him a pat on the head and send him out with your usual 'fetch'.

If, despite your precautions, the puppy does get up before you get back to him, block his way, catch him, take him back, drop him again where he started from and leave him dropped there while you go and pick the object up yourself. Never upset him if you can avoid it. Without frightening him you should not let him retrieve the object under these cir-cumstances. Although, so far as you have taught him at present, he has not committed any fault in going to retrieve without orders, he has committed an offence by leaving his drop and it is this fault that you should not condone.

If, however, circumstances are too strong for you and the puppy slips past you, do not run after him but treat the matter as if the puppy had done all right. Next time be more careful to prevent his going out until told. Throw the object when standing at the puppy's side while you gently hold him down with your other hand. If you do frighten the puppy, do not command to retrieve. Avoid this particular mistake.

From time to time, throw the dummy and go and pick it up yourself, leaving the puppy at the drop and not letting him get up until you give him permission. As soon as you can rely upon your puppy not going out to retrieve without orders, gradually increase the distance you go from him before you throw the object. Alter the direction from time to time. The spot on which the object lands should always be such as will ensure that the puppy will have to use his nose to find the object. Subject to this, it is at first a good plan to throw the object in a way which will enable your puppy to follow its general direction. Thus you will be laying the foundation for 'marking' the fall. These lessons can be varied. Go out of sight of the puppy before you throw the object. You can also begin to teach him to work to your hand or start to lay trails for him to follow.

In all these lessons, never send your puppy to retrieve until you have come right back to him and given him the command. If he leaves his drop without orders, never fail to put him back in the exact spot and to go away from him at least as far as you went originally before coming back and letting him go.

At all times, the relationship between pupil and master must be one of close friendship and confidence, both enjoying the lessons. The commands must not be fierce and sympathy must be shown in the tone of voice—otherwise a 'cowed' pupil will result.

Other Methods of Teaching Retrieving

Forced retrieving should be avoided. So long as your spaniel is not too old to learn, the initial retrieving lessons indicated in the last chapter are applicable to puppies or dogs of any age. If, however, they are postponed longer than early puppyhood days your dog will have developed a will and ideas of his own.

If your dog will pick up the object you have thrown for him but despite all your adroitness will not come back to you with it, you must use the check-cord. Let this be light, but strong. You will find that super-woven line answers this description and that lengths between five and ten yards long do not knot.

Let your dog trail the check-cord for a few days to get accustomed to it, and sometimes lead him by it. Throw the object as you would have done to your puppy, and when he gets firmly hold of it gently play the dog up to you with the check-cord as you would a fish, walking or running slowly away as recommended in the last chapter, and giving praise. Gradually make less and less use of the cord but keep it on for some time so that in case your dog shows his old disinclination to come up to you you still have the cord to fall back on. A narrow passage can also serve the same purpose as a check-cord.

The method employed in these lessons so far has been to start by throwing something for the dog to fetch, and then to induce him with or without a check-cord to bring it back to you. There is, however, another quite distinct method which starts from the other end of the business. It consists in first getting the dog to walk by your side while carrying the object in his mouth, and you do not start throwing an object for the dog to retrieve until he is perfect in this. You must first get your dog to walk to heel on a very light and short cord—a piece of salmon line meets the case—and to stop at command. In the fullness of time, dangle the object you have selected for this lesson before the dog until he takes it from your hand. Make it a pleasure for him to do so. If he will pick it up from the ground let him. When one object is perhaps distasteful to the dog, you must try another and another until you hit upon the right one, just as is recommended in the case of a young puppy which refuses to pick up the knotted pocket handkerchief. If you have a trained dog that will readily take and carry the object, have him out and give it him to carry for the example and encouragement of the novice. Again jealousy can prove profitable.

As soon as your novice takes the object from your hand, continue to walk on with him for a few yards and then stop him. Put your hand down very quietly, as any sudden movement will probably make the dog drop the object; then stroke his back. Repeat this walking, stopping and stroking two or three times before you take the object, and when you do take it be careful to take it by putting you hand underneath his jaws and pressing the object upwards and towards rather than away from his mouth, at the same time telling him 'dead'.

It is perhaps hardly necessary to say that the reason why you do not take the object from the dog every time you stop him is that you do not want him to regard it as a matter of course that whenever he stops he is to give the object up. If you keep him in uncertainty as to whether on any particular stop he is to give the object up or not, he is less likely to fall into the objectionable habit of dropping it on the ground. If he does drop the object from time to time and seems disinclined to pick it up, pick it up yourself, let him take it from your hand and, without moving from the spot, take it straight from his mouth. Dogs under training by this method are generally those which are not by nature keen on lifting or carrying anything, and on this account are apt to drop their dummy. In time, you will of course dispense with a cord and make the dog walk to heel while carrying the object, and will stop him occasionally and sometimes take the object—and sometimes not. Never make him carry the object far without taking it from him. If he gets tired of it, he will drop it, just the thing you want to avoid. At all times offer praise and encouragement. Never be harsh or temperamental for this can be disastrous.

As soon as you find that he will carry the object while at your side and hold it until you take it from him, throw the object for him to fetch and continue his retrieving lessons in

the manner previously suggested, taking particular care to
let the dog come up from behind you to the position of 'heel'.
You should also keep him waiting before you take the object
from him. Now and then, make him walk at heel with it, and
stop once or twice before you let him give it up. This lesson
serves two purposes. It encourages retrieving, and teaches
the pupil to walk to heel.

If the dog refuses to take any object from your hand, your
only course will be to open his mouth as gently as possible
and put the object into it and hold it there. Repeat this action
whenever he drops it; repeat, repeat, repeat; firmly but
kindly. If even this fails, you had better get rid of the dog if
retrieving is a *sine qua non*. Although there is still another
method of teaching retrieving, generally called the French
method of forced retrieving, this is only likely to be successful in
the hands of an accomplished trainer for whom these notes
are not intended. In the hands of a novice it is almost sure to
entail unnecessary hardship on the dog and result in failure
and frustration. At no time must punishment be connected
with the physical act of retrieving. Otherwise a faulty
delivery will result.

Assuming that by the employment of one or other of the
methods suggested in this chapter you have overcome your
dog's disinclination to pick up the object and bring it back
to you, his subsequent education can be carried out on the
lines indicated earlier. He must be taught to drop to command
and hand and stay where dropped until told to go, to use his
nose, to wait for orders before going out to retrieve, and, if
there are the necessary facilities, to drop to fur or feather.

All the suggestions for teaching these and other matters
mentioned in the last chapter can be adopted in the same
way as if you had successfully taken your dog in hand in
early puppyhood. Unless, however, your dog is an excep-
tionally shy one, you can relax to a slight extent your
scrupulous attention to the rule against any display of
harshness.

Dropping to Shot

Dropping to shot is the Basis for Steadiness in the Field

Having by the graduated series of lessons suggested in Chapter 4 taught your dog to drop to hand, it is a very short step to getting him to drop to shot. Buy a blank revolver and blank cartridges. Load your revolver, up-raise the pistol hand and snap off a cartridge as you do so. If the dog is looking towards you when you raise your hand he will probably be down at the moment you fire. If he is looking the other way, he will turn towards the noise and seeing the up-raised hand, will as usual drop to the well-known signal. In time he connects the shot with dropping and goes down whenever he hears it, whether you raise your hand or not. Dropping to shot is the basis of all control and steadiness.

Although spaniels are not often troubled with gun-shyness, at any rate permanently, it is best to be on the safe side. Prior to beginning the above lessons get your dog accustomed to the noise of the report by snapping off your pistol at some distance from his run, or getting an attendant to do so. If the dog shows any signs of nervousness put off the dropping to shot lessons until, by having the gun snapped off at a gradually decreasing distance from the dog or as a signal for meal-times, and by making much of him by way of encouragement, you have dispelled all trace of nervousness.

If your dog be shy or nervous of the shot wait until he strikes a hot scent before firing; he may then be so keen on his hunting that the shot loses its power to shock him. Another very successful method with a gun-shy dog is to wait until he is very hungry and then fire the blank off while he is eating. Start a distance away and repeat often.

Answering to Whistle and 'Back'

When you come to shooting over your puppy, you do not want to spend the day with an artificial whistle between your lips. Although it is useful to have such a whistle in your pocket or hung on your coat as a last resort, you will have to rely in the main on the whistle sound produced by your own unaided mouth and it is this sound or rather combination of sounds that is here referred to. Nothing disturbs game so much as the human voice and you must therefore teach your puppy to answer to your whistle.

The occasions on which you will want to whistle to your dog may be divided roughly into (a) when you want to attract his attention, e.g., to turn him when he is hunting and you wish him to leave scent and (b) when you want him to come back to you. It is most useful to have two different notes or combination of sounds for these two different occasions; e.g., a single low whistle for the one and a more compelling series of notes (something like that produced by a pea whistle) for the other. A Girl Guide's or Boy Scout's whistle is ideal to use as a stop whistle.

Teaching your dog to come back to you when you whistle presents no difficulty. Drop your dog, walk on leaving him dropped while seeing that he does not move even an inch. Having gone some little distance, whistle him up. When he comes to you give him rewarding praise. Up till now, you have never let your dog leave his drop until you have gone back to him. If because of the training he received in former lessons he does not come to your whistle, call him by name and encourage him to come up to you.

You must be careful not to overdo these coming-in whistle lessons. If you do, he will gradually lose his steadiness at drop. For every time that you whistle him up from his drop, at least twice as often make him stay dropped by hand until you return to him. When he has learned the meaning of your whistle, which he should very soon do, do not drop him before whistling him up, but seize occasions when he is some way from you and reward him whenever he comes up readily by encouragement and praise.

In connection with these lessons it is useful to teach your dog the meaning of the word 'back' in preparation for his lessons in hunting. When you are out with your dog on a road, let him go on in front of you, and then stand still and give him the command 'back'. Supplement this new command with his name and give him praise when he gets back to you. If desired, the use of this word may be subsequently dropped, and the dog taught to come back and hunt nearer to you by a less compelling variation of your 'come in' whistle.

A low whistle should be used to attract your dog's attention. Definite lessons for this are generally unnecessary as the dog soon understands what the low whistle means when it comes to hunting. If thought necessary you can give your low whistle supplemented by his name, and when the dog is near you offer him praise. You can also throw your reward on the ground away from your dog, give your whistle, and work the dog up to it.

Take time to finish. Let natural ability develop its own pace. Many of the lessons may have been given in a paddock so far, or even on a lawn. There is no reason why a puppy of six months should not by now have received a perfect preliminary education although his trainer may not have had access to a single acre of shooting. The necessary commands are understood, the puppy will drop to hand and shot and possibly fur, remain at drop until told to go, retrieve a dummy rabbit at a gallop right up to hand, and wait for orders.

Those who have spaniel ground at their doors, should let the puppy grow up with his work, and from the beginning give him at odd moments, the chance of getting scent into his nose. He will thus be encouraged to face cover, and be gaining some idea of hunting to his master. In other words, most of the suggestions as to hunting contained in Part Three will have been carried out before the handtraining of Part Two has been completed. Any chance of the puppy chasing should be avoided. You do not want to quarrel with the puppy in these early days, but a chase left unrebuked means trouble in the future.

PART THREE
Subsequent Training

6

'A Natural Retriever is a Gem Beyond Price'

Having completed the handtraining laid down in Part Two the dividing line between handtraining and work in the field gradually disappears. It is well, therefore, either before or during your lessons on hunting, to carry his retrieving lessons from the dummy rabbit up to the real article. This is a step that I personally always take with a certain amount of trepidation and I endeavour to make the change gradually. Your dummy rabbit has been a cold and stiff object and your first real rabbits and birds should also be cold and stiff to lessen the shock your dog will receive on coming up to the unaccustomed object. Also put your dummy rabbit in a fixed spot for a time or two and follow this by putting your first cold rabbits or birds in that same spot.

Take care that your first game is small as well as cold and that it is free from any external blood. Place it so that the back of the game will first present itself to the dog as he comes up to it, for you want him to carry it well in his mouth and not by the skin or feathers. With the sole exception of the object, nothing else should be changed. Whistle him up to you if he has grown accustomed to this. Stand still or retreat as the case may be, and take the game from him in exactly the same way as you have acted in the case of the dummy.

Continue the lessons with cold game until he brings it as well as he did the dummy. Then change to one that you have just killed and placed for him to bring; the next step is to go on to one that he has seen you shoot when at heel, finishing up with one that he has found himself. To begin with each rabbit or bird you send him for should be dead and have ceased kicking.

The system suggested above, of placing any object new to the dog in a spot from which he is accustomed to retrieve, can be applied to every species of feather he will be called upon to retrieve in the field. It is especially useful to counteract the dislike so many dogs have of lifting woodcock and snipe.

For several reasons I suggest carrying on the above lessons with pigeons. Partridges will probably not be available at the time of year you want to introduce him to his real business, and even if available are not generally so easily come by as pigeons. If you prefer partridges, and circumstances permit, by all means start on them and come to pigeons later.

On the subject of laying trails, trainers of retrievers and spaniels are not in entire agreement. Some trainers avoid trails altogether and consider their own foot-scent an efficient substitute. Some never lay them with the retrieving bundle, but wait until such time as the puppy has had his first lessons in retrieving the real article and lay them with that. Others lay them with a bundle slightly scented with aniseed, while some lay the retrieving bundle pure and simple.

In deciding for yourself this question of laying your trails you must remember that you have to train your spaniel to ignore most foot-scents when he is hunting. Consequently, you must have some means of teaching him, on receiving the appropriate command, to change his tactics when you wish him to pick up and follow the foot-scent of wounded fur or feather. Whether you use a dead pigeon or rabbit, a skin or a bundle, it is long odds that if you drag it by your side, your dog will stand your own line rather than the one you have laid for him. When laying trails, from time to time carry the object instead of dragging it and watch the result.

Although the ability to take your own foot-scent at a gallop may have some value, it leaves much to be desired. Various devices have therefore been adopted with the object of avoiding confusion of your own scent with that of the object dragged. It may suffice, for a time at least, to get someone else to drag the object in the ordinary manner. Let him get well away before you bring up your dog. On the other hand, you may by juggling with a long line, a series of posts or trees and a wide detour on your own part succeed in laying a trail some distance away from your own. Simpler still, you can attach the object to the end of a fishing rod by a short piece of string and by this means trail the object at a little distance from your own foot-scent, but if you desire to make assurance doubly sure, get someone else to lay the trail with this.

If it appeals to you, you can teach your dog to go back for anything that you have dropped, whether he has seen you drop it or not. Incidentally, this teaches him to stick to the line of your own foot-scent. Drop the object, at first in his sight and afterwards unknown to him, and take him along with you for an ever increasing distance before you send him back for it. This is said to cultivate the memory. It is certainly most useful in hurrying up a dog that is getting slow in his return, for he will not like being left behind. This method also considerably improves a tender-mouthed dog that tends to keep dropping the object on the return journey.

It is not my intention to dwell at length upon your spaniel's introduction to the various phases of the retrieving business. There are many excellent books on retrievers and what is sauce for one is sauce for the other. A few hints may however be useful.

Never send a young dog to retrieve feather unless you are sure that it is down, and to begin with, that it is dead. This advice also applies to a rabbit unless you are sure that it is either killed or so disabled as to be unable to reach its burrow. You want to impress upon your dog that the stuff is there to find if only he looks long enough. Do not send him for every-thihg you kill. Never shoot a rabbit he has found unless he drops.

Do not shoot too close, and as a result damage game.

If your dog is at fault and looks back to you for guidance, treat him as a man and a brother and do your best to help him from where you stand.

Finally, do not reiterate 'hie lost'. If you have trained him properly, he should know the meaning of the word as well as you. Repetition of it is useless for it makes him look a fool, and if he pays any attention to such a reiterated 'hie lost' this distracts his mind from the business he has in hand. His concentration is thus broken so do try at all times to let him solve his own problems.

Teach the dog to concentrate on the problem without interference of voice or whistle. Only as a last resort, when failure is in sight, come to his assistance with hand signals or directions and then only if you are very confident of the answer yourself—for so often the dog is right and you are wrong.

7

Hunting

In Cover

Style and Pace are a Joy to Behold

A spaniel that will not hunt gorse, bramble and other punishing cover is not worthy of the name. These are just the very places where his utility is most conspicuous and in which a good dog is well-nigh indispensable. It is also a part of a spaniel's work in which puppies, even of the same litter, differ to a surprising extent.

Some puppies seem to have inherited this knowledge, but the others will have to be taught or allowed to discover that it is in such sanctuaries that game is to be found. It is not probable that a spaniel loves thorny places or desires prickles any more than you or I. Only when he has learnt that they hold what his soul desires, the scent of fur or feather, does his enthusiasm rise superior to our own. The way to teach him to work the thick is not to push or pitch him into it but to show him that it is game-holding cover and leave the rest to him. In the absence of rabbits, this is extremely difficult.

A spaniel that is accustomed to work and find only on open ground is not likely to quest among what he has grown to believe are unprofitable thorns. You must first teach him that they often hold the game, and you can best do so by the usual appeal to his appetite, and by beginning as before with easy work.

Take your puppy to some standing bracken or other high prickleless cover. Throw in a bit of biscuit, let him see you do so and tell him to 'get in'. Gradually extend his investigations to more forbidding-looking cover, usually selecting that through which there is a run. In his investigations after biscuit he will from time to time find game, and after having once learnt that game is to be found therein should never thereafter be shy of prickly cover. An old dog which is keen on rough ground is a very useful adjunct in teaching these lessons. Send him to where game is likely to be found and your puppy will soon follow. Try and use the wind to the advantage of the pupil.

In the absence of rabbits, greater use of an experienced dog is advisable to set an example and to give a lead. Autumn and winter are much easier for the youngsters as cover is not so dense, the leaf is off and brambles die. The clinging 'green' bramble is the cover detested by pups. I repeat, always plan to hunt into the wind.

In the Open

We have seen that working in the open, a spaniel should hunt all the ground within twenty yards on each side of the gun—first hunting all likely cover on one side, then crossing in front of the handler while still hunting, and then working on the other side and back again until he finds or the beat is finished. This should be done up or down wind, at the best pace of which the dog is capable without over-running his nose, without unduly dwelling on foot-scents—and without missing any ground and without a word or whistle from his handler.

How to bring about this result is the problem you have to face. Up to the present, you have not given any handtraining lessons directed to this object, and in consequence you will find that the inculcation of a proper method of hunting takes more time than preventing your dog chasing or retrieving without orders. It is also the part of your dog's education in which you will have to rely to a greater extent upon your own judgement as applied to the particular dog you are training. The following notes must therefore be taken as the merest suggestions.

The first question that presents itself is as to whether you are to give the first lessons on ground where there is no scent and nothing to find, or on ground where there is a certain amount of game. Places where there is likely to be much game can be ruled out at once. You do not want to be under the necessity of continually dropping your dog and so checking him in his work. Nor do you want your dog to think that he must be continually finding game and so lapse into the habit of 'chucking it' if he does not find soon.

The practice of spaniel trainers varies materially, I believe, on this question of ground. Some start quartering lessons on bare grass, force their puppies to make short beats and rely upon pace, style, keenness and use of nose coming later. Some use a check-cord and some do not.

Personally I prefer ground where there is something for the dog to find; endeavour to do without the check-cord, and rely mostly upon showing him that the handler is helping him to attain his object and pleasure in life; i.e., the finding of game, and consequently that you are not acting merely as an arbitrary taskmaster.

The chief difficulties you will encounter at the start are (1) preventing the dog going straight out in front of you instead of quartering his ground, (2) preventing his going out too far on each side of you or, in the case of some puppies, getting him to go out far enough; and (3) preventing him dwelling on unprofitable foot-scent. It is in order to meet these difficulties that it has been suggested in previous chapters that you should teach your dog to distinguish between your low whistle which means 'back' and your 'gone away' signal.

In the earlier lessons be sparing of any command likely to check the dog unless he is a very bold one and do not insist upon too exact a compliance with your wishes in the matter of method of working his ground. These lessons, like the handtraining lessons, must be made easy at first, and then very gradually worked up to the point of instant and absolute obedience. They should culminate in your dog's ability to work his ground entirely on his own.

The ground-work of your lessons on a proper method of working—for want of a better word herein called quartering —is the inclination of your dog to follow you wherever you go, and his natural instinct, if he has it, to quarter the wind.

Start your beat therefore straight into the wind and quarter it yourself in short beats. By holding your hand out, preferably not very far from the ground, and other encouragements, get your dog out beyond you in the direction across the wind that you are going. As soon as he has got out, give your low whistle and turn sharply in the contrary direction across the wind and hold your hand out in the new direction. As soon as your dog has come across you and gone out beyond you, turn again sharply across the wind, give your whistle, get your dog across and beyond you, and repeat these movements until the end of the beat. This sounds rather complicated but the general idea may be gathered from diagram No. 1, in which the thick lines approximately represent your own track and the dotted lines those of your dog. Your beat begins from the bottom of the diagram on page 95.

If you can arrange your beat so that somewhere near each of the points, A, A, A, A, A, etc., there is a small gorse bush, small patch of rushes, bracken or other likely cover, you will make your task the easier. In your lessons on hunting thick cover you will have taught your dog that these are the places where game is to be found. If, in addition to holding your hand towards them, you give your well-known 'get in', it is more than likely that your dog will race across you towards the first of them. Having worked it, he will turn to your whistle the more readily when he sees that you are directing him to another similar patch.

If your dog will not turn to your low whistle, you will have to call him by name or resort to your more compelling human

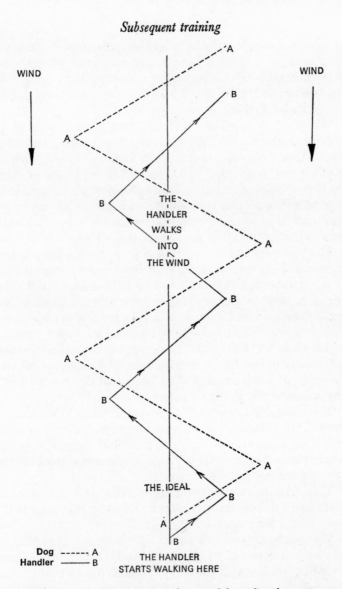

Diagram 1. First quartering and hunting lessons

or artificial whistle such as 'back' or 'turn now' or 'hey' or some expression that catches the dog's attention when he has to turn. Each time that he begins to turn to this, repeat your low whistle. It is this low whistle that you want your dog to connect with turning.

You may also find it useful to 'start' your dog hunting with your low whistle, at the same time holding out your hand. Also, from time to time, take him within ten yards or so of a rough patch that he knows and start him into it with the low whistle and pointing hand combined. This should help him to connect your low whistle with game-holding cover and teach him to understand that when he hears it he must turn to you for direction as to where the cover is.

The plans set out in Diagram No. 1 are only intended to explain the general nature of your first lessons in quartering. It is not intended that it should be followed in detail. The angles of your own quartering may be more or possibly less acute. You may find that you can get your dog to go well out from you across the wind without making your own quarterings so long; and I sincerely hope that your dog will not, at any rate after the first lesson or two, quarter with the regularity shown by the dotted lines. If he does, and the ground holds any scent, he has probably got no nose.

The greater the tendency your dog displays to work on in front of you instead of quartering his ground, the more acute you should make the angle of your own quarterings—in other words the more closely you should come back on the line of your last previous beat.

This, and the fact that you are working up wind which at first should be your invariable rule, should go far to meet the first of your difficulties.

The tendency to work on straight ahead should also be further counteracted by the use of your 'back'. Up to now, your dog has learned that this command means that he is to come straight back to you. If whenever you use it when he is hunting, you hold your hand to one side with an inclination somewhat behind you, he will soon learn that it means that he is not necessarily to come straight back to you but is only to hunt nearer to you on the side your hand indicates.

As your dog gradually gets to understand what is required of him, make your own quarterings shorter and shorter until at last you are walking in a straight line up your beat with your dog quartering his ground and working a strip at least thirty yards wide—with yourself in the middle (Diagram No. 2). Always keep him going at a gallop, even if you have to run yourself. Although a spaniel should know where his trainer is and work accordingly, he should go at the gallop all the time and only see his trainer out of the corner of his eye. Whenever he stops to see where you are, whistle him across you. Keep him bustling all the time.

Of the difficulties mentioned earlier the third has not yet been dealt with, i.e. preventing your dog dwelling on unprofitable scent, generally foot-scent, and so getting into the habit of 'pottering'. If, as I suggest, you are giving your hunting lessons on ground where there is a probability of your dog finding something, there is sure to be a certain amount of scent—and even if it is only a rabbit run your dog, we hope, is equally sure to acknowledge this scent. On the one hand you do not want him to take up a line that leads to a burrow perhaps a quarter of a mile away. On the other hand you do want to encourage by every possible means his thirst for any scent that may lead to game, or even up to game that is moving on a yard or two in front of his nose.

This being so, your action when your dog acknowledges a scent during these early lessons, must depend partly upon the natural qualities of the particular dog you are training and partly upon whether you consider the scent likely to be profitable or not. If the dog is dwelling upon what is obviously a run or place which clearly cannot hold any game, call him off immediately with your 'gone away' and hunt him away from it. If there is any doubt about the matter, call the dog off immediately if he is inclined to potter. How-

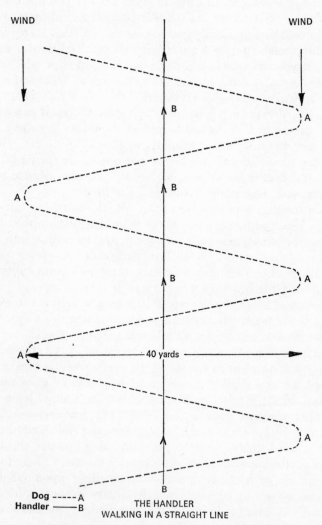

Diagram 2. Final quartering lessons

ever, if he is a naturally fast and keen worker, you can give him more time to investigate the scent, and so decide the matter for himself. The safest rule is, I think, to err on the side of calling off your dog too soon rather than on that of letting him dwell upon the scent too long. Pottering in a gundog is an abomination to be avoided at all hazards.

If you experience much difficulty in getting your dog to turn to your low whistle, it is not a bad plan to take him on to ground where there is no scent. Start him off, still up wind and to one side of you. Only let him go out a few yards on each beat before insisting on his turning to your whistle, gradually letting him out farther as he improves in this respect. A dog will often turn to command at five yards away, although he refuses to do so at fifteen. In this, as in all other lessons, the rule should be that the nearer the dog is to you the more subdued should be your whistle or your voice. If you habitually shout at a dog that is near you, you will need a megaphone to enforce your commands when he is far away.

Check-Cord

If despite all your ingenuity your dog still refuses to turn to your low whistle fairly consistently, you will as a last resort have to hunt him on a ten to twenty yard long check-cord and turn him by this means, using your low whistle as an accompaniment to the pull of the cord. The best material for the cord, as stated in an earlier chapter, is a thin variety of what is known in the trade as 'super woven line'. Although this is strong and light it does not kink because it is woven instead of twisted. Nevertheless, the cord will be a continuous vexation to you. If you hold the end, your dog will wrap it round a clump of rushes or get it caught up in some other obstruction. If you let it go free, the end will never be anywhere near you when you want to catch hold of it to turn your dog. It will get caught up. Sometimes you will step on it yourself and bring your dog to a full stop just as he is beginning to go nicely, and thus by creating chaotic confusion in his mind, make him go in a hesitating and uncertain manner and check all pace and dash. With this picture of horror before you and its dire accompaniment of loss of temper on your part, postpone using the cord until every other expedient has failed. If you have once been driven to it, I am sure no words of mine will be needed to induce you to dispense with it as soon as possible.

Dropping

As soon as your dog goes out readily and quarters fairly and freely, make a point of dropping him and leaving him dropped a minute or two before you start him hunting. Then give him the signal to hunt, give a click of your tongue and a hand direction to show him whether he is to go out to right or left. If you are training two puppies and are likely in the future to work them as a brace, it is useful to accustom one always to start out on the right and the other always to start out on the left.

As your dog improves in his quartering, drop him by command and subsequently by shot from time to time—but not too often to bore him—sometimes when near you, sometimes when well out, sometimes on the outward and sometimes on the inward tack. See that he drops without hesitation and does not move until you start him off again with your low whistle or 'gone away': 'Gone away' wants developing to perfection by repetition. It cannot be too often pointed out that this dropping instantaneously wherever he may be is the foundation of steadiness. If he will not do so when there is no strong counter-attraction, you will never get him to do so when a rabbit is legging it in front of him.

Chasing

This brings us to the question of what you are to do when in the course of his lessons on hunting he flushes game.

If his handtraining has been finished off by teaching him to drop to flush as suggested in Part 2, there is no reason why he should not of his own accord drop to the first game he finds. Most of my own puppies do so. There will, however, possibly come a time when he throws all his handtraining lessons to the wind. This will probably occur when he has got on to the scent of game that is moving along in front of him in such cover as rushes. Both dog and game are on the move and in the same direction. The dog is gradually overtaking the game. Eventually the game moves in earnest and your dog's feelings get the better of him. The trainer should try to anticipate the break or flush.

Whenever your dog fails to drop on his own account, you must do your best to drop him to command. If despite your attempts a chase occurs, stand still and wait until the dog comes back. If he has been well trained up to this point, he will have his tail between his legs in acknowledgement of his fault. Take hold of him, drag him to the exact spot where he should have dropped, go some distance from him— I usually sit down and light a pipe—leaving him dropped for a minute or two at least or longer if he seems unrepentant, and I do not let him leave his drop until I have gone back to him. In the case of an obstinate but nervous dog, the 'taking hold of him' may be the rub. If this difficulty occurs, in future hunt him with a short check-cord only just long enough to enable you to get him up to you. A length of a yard or two should suffice, and this should be kept on until you find you can dispense with it.

Hunting Down-wind

So far nothing has been said about hunting down-wind. The reason for recommending that all the first lessons in quartering should be given up-wind is as follows. When working down-wind, a spaniel's inclination is to draw out straight in front of you instead of quartering his ground, and to get out too far. This tendency is much more pronounced down-wind and it may be the dog's desire to get away from your scent has a lot to do with this.

Until he quarters his ground fairly well up-wind it is most important not to ask him to hunt down-wind except at rare intervals and then for not long at a time. When you do begin the down-wind lessons, be particularly careful to start him off to one side as usual and try to get him well out—in this way you will counteract his tendency to turn sooner than usual and to go straight down-wind instead of crossing you. If this tendency asserts itself, stand still. Give your usual 'back' and work him by your hand towards and across you. Do not walk on until he has got level with you. At the same time do not let him work behind you into the wind unless he is obviously on a scent.

The most effective method of working a spaniel down-wind is a matter of opinion. Personally, I do not object to him going well out down-wind and working his ground up-wind back to me. If he works down-wind in the same way as up, I am generally suspicious of his nose.

It is unreasonable to expect that same pace or efficiency in a spaniel quartering down-wind as in a spaniel working up-wind. In the former case he has to search for a scent—in the latter it is coming on the wind straight to his nose. Similarly, you should not expect your spaniel to go at the same pace at all times on all ground. One day and place may be good scenting and another bad. A good dog knows this and regulates his pace accordingly.

If your dog goes well both up-wind and down-wind, a cross-wind does not present much difficulty. In a diagonal head-wind he will, however, naturally quarter the wind and it is well to prevent his quartering taking him too much behind you. To prevent this, whistle him across when on such a track sooner than you would if the direction of the beat were straight into the wind.

Hunting within Gunshot

In all quartering lessons, especially up-wind, aim at whistling your dog across as soon as ever he has reached the limit you have set for the distance he is to go out from you—and stick to this limit. A spaniel must spring his game within gunshot of you, and the length of his quartering has consequently to be determined with reference to you and not the nearest hedge or wall. This turning to whistle is only a prelude to the dog turning at the proper distances on his own initiative. If you whistle him across sometimes at five yards and sometimes at fifty he will never get a proper range confirmed and you will have to whistle him across to the end of the chapter.

Your eye will soon tell you when your dog has got out as far as you like him to go. If, whenever he gets to about this distance, you whistle him across you he will in time learn to turn at the same distance of his own accord. Do not, however, trust too soon in his having acquired a confirmed range, and even after you think he has acquired one whistle him across from time to time. Very few dogs are so good as not to require a whistle to turn them on occasions, and the obedience to your low whistle learned in his early days may easily be lost and forgotten through disuse.

Hunting, Missing Ground

When your dog has once learned to quarter his ground fairly well, take special care that he does not miss any ground that is likely to hold game. If you see that he has not brought, say, a small gorse bush within range of his nose, do not go up to it and kick up any rabbit or game it may hold but insist upon your dog coming back to investigate it himself. When out 'spanielling', and even at field trials, there is nothing more annoying than to see your dog baulked off a find by some officious foot.

Hunting, in Hedgerow

The reader will no doubt have gathered from the above observations, if his own experience has not already so taught him, that the proper working of open ground is not easily attained. The difficulty of attaining it is only equalled by the ease with which it may be lost. Do not therefore risk its loss in the early days by allowing your dog to indulge in his inclination to go out in front of you which, for example, he must of necessity do when working a hedge. Useful as this accomplishment may be on many rough shoots, postpone it until he has acquired a confirmed range. At any rate, during his first season use him for it sparingly.

Most dogs have an inborn love of hedge-hunting and this may be useful to you in testing your spaniel's obedience in turning to whistle. You may work him on a beat bounded on one side by a hedge and let him work a few yards of the hedge before you whistle him across, but insist that he obeys.

When the time is ripe for hedge work, you should find your 'get in' enough to induce your dog to work it from your own side. You may, however, desire to teach him to work from the far side. In such cases select a hedge over or through which you can see him. Get him across with 'over' (throwing a piece of biscuit will soon teach him the word); stop him when he has got far enough ahead of you and make him wait until you get almost abreast of him and have given him leave to go on. In a short time, an intelligent dog will from the far side put his head through every gap or thin place in the thickest hedge to find out where you are, and will wait until you come up with him. If the dog comes through to your side of the hedge without orders, make him get back the same way as he came.

As you are on one side of the hedge and your dog is on the other, you are of course powerless to prevent him going right ahead unless you have previously taught him to stop on command. You can if you like drop him in your usual way. Your inability, however, to enforce his dropping if he disobeys, is likely to weaken his obedience to that command. It is better to use a distinct command such as the hiss. Every time he disobeys this, call him in and make him stop under circumstances where no prickly hedge prevents you from enforcing your commands.

8

Hunting with the Gun

Experience with Live Scent is all-important

The foregoing notes cover, I think, all single work except the carrying and use of the gun. During the earliest lessons on quartering, it is no use hampering yourself with anything more bulky than your Belgian revolver and a few blank cartridges. You will want the blanks when continuing the lessons on dropping to shot, but until your dog quarters boldly, be sparing of their use. If before this period arrives he gets slack about dropping to shot, continue his lessons in dropping to shot but only when you are not hunting him, so as to avoid the risk of cramping his style.

The period at which you begin to carry a gun when hunting, will depend largely upon the dog. You will soon discover whether he goes better with a gun or without, and will act accordingly. Whichever way it might be, your ultimate aim is to get him to go equally well in either case. Do not therefore always carry a gun. On the other hand, do not always be without one. At field trials for spaniels, the trainer is not allowed to shoot but is allowed to carry a gun if he so desires. It is, however, an awful nuisance lugging a gun about all day as well as your dog. It is well therefore to get your dog to work to you and not to your gun. If he is not accustomed to this, you will find that at field trials he will work to the gun carried by the official shooters who are appointed to shoot the game and not to you. On that account he will be more difficult to handle and will be apt to miss much of the ground on your allotted beat.

When you have a gun in your hand use it to drop your dog in lieu of your pistol. This is to say drop him to it from time to time when there is nothing to shoot at. In no case shoot anything unless your dog has dropped to it or has not seen it. It is one thing for your dog to be steady to a rabbit going away unharmed, and quite another thing for him to remain at his drop when he sees it suddenly bowled over—in legal phrase 'reduced into possession'. For this reason, do not shoot game to him when hunting until you have many times let off your gun wide of the game that he has started, and he has been cured of any inclination to run into the combined effect of the game and the shot.

When you do begin to shoot to him, do not let him retrieve the first kill. Leave him dropped, go and pick up the rabbit or game yourself, and then come back to him with it and do not let him stir until you are ready for him to go on with his beat.

The principle that you are seeking to instil is that when you kill, your dog is not to automatically retrieve. If you send him every time he begins to connect the kill and ultimately the shot with retrieving, and disregard the intermediate step, i.e. your permission to go out.

The temptation with every novice at training is to 'practise' his dog in retrieving every time he kills or thinks he has. If there is a sure way of throwing away the fruits of all the earlier lessons, it is to give way to this temptation. Just as the maxims 'Training is only a Figure of Speech' and 'The Preliminary Course is by Far the Most Important' are essential to the making of a good spaniel, so are these other maxims, 'Do not send your dog for everything you kill' and 'Do not shoot unless your dog is down' essential if you would not mar him when made. The first of these should be observed during the whole of your spaniel's sporting career. Strict observance of the second may be confined to his earlier years.

So long as your spaniel shows the slightest inclination to

retrieve without orders, look to see whether he has dropped before you get your gun up and do not shoot if he is not down. Even if he is down, let the rabbit or game get well away before you let off your gun. A miss may result, but a few extra rabbits or game in the bag are no compensation for the spoiling of your dog.

You must not, of course, send your dog to retrieve immediately you have killed. Leave him dropped until he has thoroughly settled down. The more eager he is to go, the longer you must keep him down. The temptation to make sure of adding one more to the bag may be great but you must resist it. If you yourself have no self-control, you cannot expect your dog to acquire it. If your dog shows any inclination to go in without orders, do not let him go until you have come up to him and patted his head and, in addition, have given him your usual command.

If, despite due observance of the above maxims, you should find great difficulty in getting your dog steady to shot, do not let him hunt. Keep him at heel, and as a last resource, use a trailing check-cord. See that he drops to your shot and send him to retrieve, but seldom.

On the other hand, if your dog though steady is getting sloppy in his retrieving, only hunt him often enough to keep his hunting right. Use him as a retriever whenever opportunity offers. Many keen game-finders come to regard the retrieving business as rather a bore and are impatient to get on hunting again.

At the beginning of a season, do not expect your dog to be as good as he was at the end of the previous season. Put him through a modified course of handtraining before the season opens, for in doing this you will save much loss of time and temper and the possible ruination of your dog. When it comes to his first day in the fields, shoot over him carefully. Assume that he intends to be completely disobedient and to go in at every shot.

PART FOUR

Mixed Bag

(The Trained Spaniel at Work)

9

Retrieving from Water

Carlton said 'My lines have not been cast in a country which lends itself to the higher branches of water work'. Mine have, so I have added my own observations on this aspect.

The introduction to water should coincide with a reasonable temperature of both water and atmosphere. Age too should be taken into account before actual physical contact with water is made. I would suggest twelve to sixteen weeks of age should be the earliest age to attempt the introduction. The ideal time is a hot spell in late spring or during the remaining summer months when the pup or puppies have reached the age of exploration. I much prefer a bunch of young pups and I take them for their usual walk around the edges of a pond, lake or sea. Competition between the group soon leads to the more adventurous ones exploring the water's edge—splashing about, playing and generally enjoying the experience. The timid ones will increase their curiosity, jealousy will predominate so they too will be entering the water up to a swimming depth. If other puppies are unavailable, any older dogs will ably assist.

The best method is to accompany the pups into the water yourself. A pair of waders splashing about on the edges always attracts a puppy in. Better still, a bathing suit and a swim with the pups achieves immediate results but on no account should force be used at this introduction. Great patience must be exercised in gaining the pupil's confidence in:

(a) *Yourself*
A puppy must be fully confident that under no circum-

stances will you push him in or play a confidence trick on him. I have seen it advocated that the first introduction should be 'forcible entry' but I avoid this method like the plague.

(b) *Actually Facing Water and Swimming*

Once (a) has been achieved, rapid strides can be made forthwith. Continual walks round the edges will soon naturally result in the more adventurous ones swimming a few strokes, others soon following until they all love the experience.

At this stage every encouragement should be given to get the puppies to follow you out to deeper water, so begin to wade deeper yourself. When they have become fearless and use water as they would the land, individual attention can then be introduced by throwing a dummy to be retrieved. Starting at very easy range, the distances can gradually be increased until the pupils are swimming out as far as the trainer can throw the dummy. At this stage I find it beneficial to leave open water and throw the dummy into reeds or rushes to make the pup concentrate on the type of hunting it will have to do later on when introduced to wildfowl, searching for wounded duck etc.

If the dog will be used in estuary or foreshore shooting, the long retrieves over big stretches of water should be practised by throwing the dummy down-wind and letting it drift out with the wind further and further before the dog is sent. This method can be taken to great lengths and a naturally bold dog can be taught to swim great distances by gradually increasing length of the drift. I believe it is just as easy for a dog to swim as to walk and that really long distances over water never fatigue a dog.

However, when winter comes and the temperature lowers, I do believe a young dog seizes up across the loins after long swims or standing in very cold water. For this reason I always try to avoid giving a lot of water work in the winter to a dog in his first season. With maturity, a body build-up and age, a dog will stand any reasonable amount of work in its second season. If a dog is kept exclusively for water-work, it is advisable to keep him in a much fatter condition than you would for land work. The coating of fat does seem to help in warding off the cold.

Another important feature of water work is crossing water to retrieve from the opposite bank. A bird can be killed across a river or estuary. Having fallen on land, it can create a major problem. Unless the dog has been especially trained for this situation, he will keep hunting the water and the river bank, refusing to hunt the land beyond. This can be most annoying.

Retrieving across water often presents a young dog with unsurmountable problems unless specific training on this one point has been pursued and established as part of the overall training programme. No dog is 'finished' unless it will retrieve to command from the opposite bank of a river. The current too presents difficulties for a youngster whose immediate reaction is to fight and swim against it. With experience he will let himself be carried away, swimming across the current and landing down-stream. When the collection has been made, he will follow the same procedure on the return journey. Slow running rivers do not present such a difficult task. This familiarity can only be achieved by continual practice and acclimatization to a strong running river. It is easier for all concerned to commence training in a slower running river, but not essential.

I like to start by introducing the command 'over' which can also be used on numerous other occasions in the shooting field. Even a small ditch, stream or burn will serve to commence operations. By continually throwing a dummy to the other side, your pupil will soon learn the meaning of the word 'over'. This command can then be developed to cover greater distances until the pupil is capable of covering a fairly wide river. I would not consider developing this phase until the

H   113

pup has reached at least the age of ten to twelve months or is even older.

When greater demands are being made and the dog is being asked to face greater distances, I find it helpful to have a friend or assistant on the opposite bank who will throw the dummy well away from the water. Using the command 'Fetch' and then 'Over', your dog will soon learn that a retrieve awaits it on the bank on the far side. Try small rivers first. A canal is ideal for starting on or a small estuary on an incoming tide. A flood of suitable size can also be useful. These are all suitable locations to commence training for this particular and specialized work.

The secret of this part of the training is timing your first introduction to coincide with a hot spell of real summer weather, and not to hurry your pupil.

10

Wildfowling and Flighting with Spaniels

Spaniels on the whole are fond of working in water. Their coats vary, but given a good undercoat they can withstand hardships on the coast and marsh and here compare with most other breeds.

I have found that in very cold weather standing and waiting in twelve to eighteen inches of water for a length of time puts a spaniel out of action quicker than anything else, but then it does to most other gundogs. If, while waiting, the spaniel can be left on dry land he will continue to make repeated retrieves from cold sea, lake or flash. It appears to be the waiting in freezing water that paralyses them across the loins.

It is tempting to measure the enjoyment of wildfowling by the size of the bag. I believe this to be a completely false way of judging the pleasure it can give, for so many other interesting, delightfully thrilling spectacles occur which influence the overall enjoyment. I never tire of another dawn breaking, another sunrise whatever the colour, and of watching the birth of another day, a new day full of the variations of life opening on to still unknown opportunities, tragedies and human endeavours—one more day to live, one less in our span. You become conscious of a great desire to make the most of it. The actual creeping light from the horizon produces a really tremendous feeling of awe and you feel confronted with the great power of The Almighty, at the wheel of the universe; controlling the world, space, sound, the sun and moon, all before your very eyes.

I watch as eighty or ninety whooper swans, arriving in November from their great flight from Siberia, descend in ever decreasing circles from a great height, crying like a pack of hounds in full cry. Now I call them The Hounds of Heaven and they are my constant companions. Each morning at breakfast, from November to March, they feed just across the marsh systematically grazing a field like sheep. Sometimes, wild geese join them. In a big freeze-up, large flocks of pintail, widgeon, mallard and teal stretch along the ice, sitting in the sun under the flock of whoopers and geese. These are usual scenes that make killing seem quite secondary.

Spaniels have accompanied my wildfowling all over the world: canvas-backs in Maryland, Canadian geese on the Mississippi, pink feet and grey lag in Scotland, widgeon on the Solway and duck of all descriptions on my home marsh. Rarely have the spaniels failed me.

An experienced spaniel will always see the duck coming in the dusk long before you can, so when I have a dog I know well and can trust I watch the movement of the head and immediately pick up the oncoming duck from the direction of his nose. A friend of mine had a most experienced bitch who formed the habit of sitting with her back to the oncoming duck to enable her to mark the fall behind the gun. A dog very quickly learns that incoming duck come into the wind.

I think a spaniel should be sent immediately to the fall when flighting, but the release of the dog must be controlled as it is a very short step to running into the fall. I don't allow this, but I do 'send' very quickly. An intelligent dog soon differentiates between wildfowling and other forms of shooting, where he must remain seated until the drive is over. It is all a build-up of experience. Crippled duck diving in open water create a problem for young and old dogs alike and only after encountering it repeatedly do they learn to collect under water. Floating marshes, too, present very hard going conditions so a spaniel has to have plenty of determination and stamina to last the flight. I always try and see that my dogs are dry and comfortable after one of these exhausting experiences. They have at least earned this consideration.

Flighting on flashes and pools can be great fun. In recent years, more and more of them have been regularly 'fed' with tremendous results. Unlike America where feeding is strictly prohibited, prosperous farming has provided the 'wherewithal' to make and maintain more flighting pools. Here a spaniel really comes into its own in a very short space of time. Three guns shooting on a pool will soon have plenty of duck to collect. A spaniel must be able to come in with a retrieve in his mouth while other duck fall around. Anything winged should be collected immediately, as wounded duck are capable of running great distances in a short space of time.

Morning flighting on an inland marsh can also be enthralling. The duck come for a day's rest after feeding throughout the night and when wind, weather and tide coincide, they provide wonderful sport. It is essential, however, that no late moon appears to upset the arrival time. The awakening of the marsh around one is always thrilling, different, expectant and full of interest—with, as a background, such sounds as the whistling of otters, and the call of the curlew. The first mallard drake arrives to slowly explore the surroundings, when it is too dark to even see his shadow. With his slow hoarse croak, he awaits an answering call which a clever gunner is often able to imitate—with disastrous results to the mallard. Widgeon, too, respond very well to a call. I always feel I have cheated when they hover over me looking so innocently for the caller. Cripples in over-grown marshes are extremely difficult to find and I consider it most important to get a dog out to the fall immediately.

Lending a Hand

Picking Up

One of the most important jobs on a big day is to pick up cleanly behind the guns and to clear the ground of cripples after the beaters have moved on to the next beat. More and more amateurs as well as professionals are lending a hand on the main shooting days, quite often for financial reward. To a handler with a young dog such an opportunity provides wonderful experience in the actual field. It helps in establishing steadiness and getting used to parties of guns or beaters, and offers practice in retrieving live birds, in holding lines, and collecting runners or cripples. For spaniel enthusiasts a day with the beaters, hunting, seeking and flushing game considerably assists in the build-up of experience needed to finish a good young spaniel. It also provides great fun and enjoyment to the handler or trainer as well as being a valuable contribution to the day's results.

For the guidance of the uninitiated I must outline the procedure to be followed and this advice may also help some regular pickers-up who flagrantly break the unwritten laws, thereby unintentionally causing considerable annoyance to the host, the guns and the head keeper. The golden rule is never to be late at the meet. If this is unavoidable a previous word with the host or head keeper saves misunderstanding. On arrival you will be directed to your allotted position which you should find with the least disturbance possible. On arrival don't let your dogs foul your host's lawn or the meeting place. A short run at home before you depart or a quick stop on suitable grass will allow the dogs to relieve themselves and arrive comfortable and ready to do a good job of work.

Your job is to melt unobtrusively into the background, and never be an embarrassment to the guns or your host. This requires care and thought. Yield not to temptation by stationing yourself with the guns and watching the proceedings for this is not good practice. Firstly, most guns don't wish to be encumbered with additional attention or conversation. The commands given to dogs distract their concentration and if a dog unintentionally moves to a fall, the handler has to speak. Shooting on a big day is a highly-skilled operation and needs tremendous thought, hard work and concentration. Therefore, it is imperative not to distract the guns' attention under any circumstances whatsoever, so the position of handler and dogs while the drive proceeds is all-important. Anybody can pick dead birds up around the peg at the stand. Cripples, however, soon take off and leave the area. So unless there is a very good reason against, the observers' position is well in the rear of the guns.

With grouse and partridge driving it is usually not difficult for the picker-up to melt into the background at least 100 yards behind the line. With pheasant shooting this is not always possible because ground in the rear of the line may well be required for the next beat—so it is most important that the handler knows the exact programme so as to avoid needlessly disturbing ground that is to come into the next or future drives. The man with good dogs who keeps well behind the line and melts unobtrusively into the background will do a really valuable job. He will collect cripples as they arrive, and when he knows the background is clear will move into the peg to pick up dead birds before moving on to the next stand.

The man standing close behind the gun will not produce nearly such good results. Runners will have run a long way off and dogs will have to travel further and so much valuable time will be lost. He is not nearly so efficient as the man in the background who picks up wounded birds as they arrive. At the end of the day it will give great satisfaction to know you have materially helped to fill the bag and that your dogs have performed well. The results of early training will be apparent and the bedding-in period will have commenced whereby a season's actual work will result in a completely trained dog emerging.

12

Jumping

Given the opportunity, most sporting dogs love to jump, so by introducing them to suitable obstacles at an early age they soon discover the power of propulsion which appears to intrigue them. In this way their muscles develop and before long jumping becomes a real joy and helps to lift the serious training on to a lighter plane. Any light-hearted diversion is valuable otherwise the actual obedience training can become dull and a bore, and teaching a dog to jump naturally fills the breach in this respect.

I like to start at sixteen to twenty weeks old with a suitable small jump which should not be at all formidable or difficult. It is important that there should be no alternative entry or exit to the jump—in other words the youngster has to jump to reach you. Any alleyway or passage is ideal if a small fence can be erected across it. I again repeat that the obstacles must be easily negotiated, with the command 'Over' given each time the pup approaches the fence until it is following you backwards and forwards jumping freely, with joy and delight. Once this stage has been reached it is an easy matter to increase the height and difficulty of each jump, but care must be taken to synchronize physical development with the size of the fence.

In the case of gundogs I like to introduce them to real barbed wire at an early age. I like them to prick themselves so they soon learn that they must make a special effort to clear the wire—and that if they do not they will be forcibly reminded of this each time by a sharp prick. This soon results in a healthy respect for barbed wire fences and a good clearing jump results.

Today most forestry plantations are enclosed by netting topped with one strand of barbed-wire. Birds falling into such a plantation have to be retrieved, and so the dog that has been taught to jump correctly makes easy work of a stiff barbed wire fence that frightens most handlers. In addition to plantation fences, barbed wire is now used extensively for holding stock, protecting crops etc., so in my everyday life a dog has to be able to deal courageously and fearlessly with these very dangerous obstacles.

Many handlers fear injury to their dogs and stop to lift them over a fence or try and induce them to find a hole to crawl under. I take the very opposite view, I contend that if you teach your pupil from an early age to respect barbed wire, to realize its danger and develop independence in dealing with it, you very, very rarely get a tear or injury.

The smaller sized dogs should also learn to climb barbed wire. This helps on the return with a heavy bird when a clear jump is perhaps too much to expect from them. The larger dog should learn to jump clearly. I do make one very definite proviso—the barbed wire must be really tight. I would never try to teach a youngster to jump loose barbed wire and I would be extremely watchful of a trained dog jumping loose barbed wire and would be ready to assist if the dog got caught up. Plain wire is excellent for the first introduction, but as soon as they are jumping well I do like to substitute barbed wire.

I can speak with authority and great experience on this particular subject as my land is surrounded by stiff barbed wire fences designed to hold Welsh Mountain ewes who can jump out of almost any enclosure. All my dogs are expected to jump these fences many times during a hard day's work and it is only on very rare occasions that they come to any serious damage. At the worst they suffer the odd very small tear perhaps once or twice a season—with a serious tear perhaps every five years. When you consider that under these conditions we handle perhaps five or six dogs daily for several days a week it must be realized the risk of serious injury is very slight, always providing the dogs have had a really good grounding on how to jump.

Stone walls too often confuse the largest and bravest of dogs, yet again this is all a matter of introduction and training until a stiff five-foot wall can be taken in their stride with a cock pheasant or hare in their mouth.

As with wire, start small and easy, gradually increasing until you obtain proficiency by continual practice. The golden rule is never to help your dogs over obstacles but always insist they make their own way. Just walk away and encourage them to follow and never go back unless the wall or fence is impossible. Dogs vary considerably in their development in this respect; some learn much quicker than others, but this really applies to all stages of a training programme and must be accepted. But do not overlook the fact that as with swimming it takes time to reach proficiency.

13

Spaniels as Beaters

It is great fun to train a team of spaniels for use as beaters on formal or informal days. One of the biggest problems now facing owners of shoots, shooting tenants and syndicates is the provision of efficient beaters to flush game. Costs are continuously increasing so the bill at the end of a big day is considerable. In most cases, the bag sold will only just pay for hired beaters. As most people shoot their coverts at least five times each season, the overall expense account for this one item can be quite a nasty surprise.

Several factors have considerably increased the difficulties, the foremost being the very thick undergrowth that has developed since the disappearance of the rabbit. In the early part of the season brambles, thorns and rough grass make the beating and flushing of reared pheasants well-nigh impossible, especially where young hand-reared birds are concerned.

Shooting dates often clash, reducing the number of beaters available on the same day and as a result keepers often lack team strength on shooting days. This may persuade them to consider using spaniels as beaters for such a plan has the advantage of being a permanent long-term policy.

Those who may consider forming a team of spaniels for use on their own shoot, or to be taken around to other shoots as a profitable as well as an enjoyable hobby, must take into account several important factors. The dogs should be a good type selected from a source in which the working capabilities have been founded and established on a firm working strain. Some of these strains can now be traced back for one hundred years so if care is taken the team should have plenty of natural ability. Strong-headed, wilful, jealous spaniels should be avoided at all costs.

The number of dogs in the team is dictated by individual requirements and accommodation. Between two and four is an ideal number to start with. Experience gained in the first season is helpful in deciding on the next increase. You can be gaining confidence, experience and results; the handler can further increase his team to suit himself and his circumstances building up by stages to 6, 8 or even 10. The elimination of retrieving in the entire team is the most important factor if a high standard of control is to be achieved. This also disposes of one of the main causes of jealousy and running-in to shot. A dog that has never been allowed to retrieve will have no desire to run to shot.

Jealousy and competition between the members of the team are the chief causes of trouble to the trainer and handler who must guard against this from the very commencement of the training. With this in view, each puppy should be encouraged to learn to hunt individually. A team playing 'follow my leader' on a shooting day would be quite useless.

Puppies allowed to hunt freely will soon develop the habit of waiting for the leading and most aggressive youngster to find the game while they watch. It is, therefore, most important for each puppy to hunt, in the first instance by itself. However, there are exceptions to this rule and if the youngsters show an inclination to hunt as a pack, without relying on each other, this should be encouraged. A sharp lookout should be kept for the strong individual who forges ahead regardless. Unless this enterprising spirit can be curbed, it may be necessary to replace this member of what is now a team. A good individual can upset the team; just as he can in ball games.

This is a hard decision as in all probability this resolute explorer is in other respects exactly what you want but he must conform to the team regardless. At the same time, each spaniel must be taught to turn back automatically on the flush, whistle or sign. A saving in training effort can be made by not insisting on the dropping to shot or dropping to the flush, which are finer points connected solely with retrieving. This simplifies the programme. The trainer can concentrate on the one important essential, hunting, and hunting as a pack.

When a reasonable standard of obedience has been attained and the handler is satisfied that his dogs are hunting well and responding to his commands and not just following the leader, then, and only then, can he commence welding them together as a team. After one full season, the team should not yield to temptation.

One of the most difficult tasks is to restrain the team when birds are running ahead of the beating line. This is a common situation which can be encountered at most drives, and so the time taken in training the pups not to hunt lines will have been well spent. Under no circumstances should a spaniel be allowed to hunt a line. Birds should be found by body-scent. The team should fan out and quarter systematically, covering a pre-arranged front according to the number of dogs in the team. Sometimes a dog prefers to hunt on the left while others choose the right. This should be encouraged until the handler knows roughly where each member is although he may be well out of sight.

If the spaniels work to these simple standards, it will avoid premature flushing and indiscriminate push-out of birds in all directions. Indeed this is the one main difficulty with spaniels—determining the direction of the bird after flushing. To overcome this problem it is advantageous to have men beating at regular intervals along with the dogs, but these intervals can be very much wider than usual because the dog team will be working in between. The team must work as part of the whole line, otherwise birds will tend to break back, an eventuality which should always be considered when spaniels are being used as beaters.

At the end of each drive, each dog should be put on slip. Under no circumstances should spaniels in the beating team be allowed to pick-up behind the stands.

The feeding, care and summer maintenance of such a team must be considerable, but after the initial training the time involved is small. Nevertheless, getting the team ready for work after the summer recess is quite a task. A good rule with all spaniels is to harden up during July and August. Worm them at the end of July. Follow with another dose at the end of August and this should see them through the season.

APPENDIX ONE

Breeding and Early Care of Puppies

Many breeders plan on the assumption that a well-known successful bitch mated to an equally well-known successful dog will produce outstanding progeny. It is of much greater importance to study a four-generation pedigree to gain background information on characteristics, good and bad, before deciding on a particular mating. In the absence of a pedigree full verbal enquiries can be made to assess the virtues required for reproduction. Then, applying the rule that the female contributes most of the requirements, a mating can be arranged. I know that this statement will be disputed by the scientists, but after thirty years' breeding I know it to be the soundest foundation for an amateur to build on. This rule is to select proven bitch lines to breed from or to select your stock from proven bitches or daughters of proven dams.

I believe you can mate a moderate bitch with a good family background to a moderate dog with a similar family background and get an outstanding pup.

I believe you can mate a top bitch to a top dog with indifferent family backgrounds and still get indifferent offspring.

I believe you can mate an outstanding dog to a moderate bitch and get uncertain progeny.

I believe the safest way to produce good trainable material is to breed into known families, keeping close family connections in each succeeding mating, always making certain you know which particular family quality you wish to reproduce. So, over the years, you will be able to forecast your next plan to strengthen the stock, eliminate weaknesses, determine size and colour, and establish and ensure train-ability. I believe that you do not need to look for outcrosses at more than five year intervals, assuming you breed one litter per annum. Breed within the families for happy and satisfying results.

Plan for spring pups. The ideal is for the bitch to whelp in February, March, April or May for this will ensure summer pups. Sun is essential for thriving litters and when six months old in October they will be able to withstand the winter months that follow and be ready to train at the close of the season.

Inoculate without fail at twelve to fourteen weeks old, with booster shots later.

Worm at six weeks and again at nine. Keep a sharp look-out for reinfestations and do not hesitate to worm again. Thereafter keep a watchful eye for tapeworm. A 'wormy' dog is an unhappy and uneasy dog who will be slothful to respond to your best training endeavours. It will have a ravenous appetite, a dull listless appearance and a colourless coat. Often the eye is the surest indicator. It must be bright—septic matter in the corner is an indicator and scratching too can indicate worms. Sometimes the hair surrounding the eye wears bare due to an infestation. The best guide is the overall appearance. It must be bright and gay, the coat must have a good sheen and the eye be as clear as crystal.

I like to confine my litters to not more than five or six although I am prepared to concede that large litters are often reared successfully. This, however, often places strain on the bitch and the feeder too has to be constantly supple-menting the mother's milk, so in the main a restricted litter is sound policy. Reduce the number of the litter at three days old, making your choice on a basis of sex, colour and size. At three to five days old dock, if necessary, and remove dew claws. At four weeks old supplement bitch's milk and provide calcium, yeast and the necessary vitamins. Feed four times daily from six weeks old reducing the feed to three times daily at twelve weeks. Continue twice daily until seven to eight months old.

APPENDIX TWO

Exercising Spaniels

Spaniels are naturally very clean dogs. If you are reasonably fair to them they will keep themselves and their kennel spotlessly clean. Ten minutes' exercise in the morning and ten minutes in the evening, suitable housing, with a regular type of food and a good supply of clean fresh water, will together establish a completely habit-forming routine. A top-draught of air on to a sleeping or resting dog is most undesirable. Within reason, they do not mind cold, windy or wet conditions when working, but they must lie warm and free from draughts. As a counter against top draughts fit a waterproof and draughtproof top over their sleeping compartment about twenty-four inches above the bed, with the kennel entrance (or run) facing away from the prevailing wind. Outside shelter from the hot sun is most desirable too. Extremes of all sorts are to be avoided, especially heat.

The early morning exercising period can also be interesting and refreshing for the owner. A fairly strict measure of control is kept when I exercise my dogs. To allow your dog or dogs to hunt a line without being checked is a short step down the slippery slope to unsteadiness. A few unofficial flushes at the end of illicit hunts encourages them to assume this can be accepted as standard practice. Before long, they are just hunting wild, for themselves instead of their handler. By judicious control without being too strict, this can be avoided.

Have fun.

Index